The Poetry of John Marston

The Metamorphosis of Pigmalions Image. And Certaine Satyres.

John Marston was born to John and Maria Marston née Guarsi, and baptised on October 7th, 1576 at Wardington, Oxfordshire.

Marston entered Brasenose College, Oxford in 1592 and earned his BA in 1594. By 1595, he was in London, living in the Middle Temple. His interests were in poetry and play writing, although his father's will of 1599 hopes that he would not further pursue such vanities.

His brief career in literature began with the fashionable genres of erotic epyllion and satire; erotic plays for boy actors to be performed before educated young men and members of the inns of court.

In 1598, he published 'The Metamorphosis of Pigmalion's Image and Certaine Satyres', a book of poetry. He also published 'The Scourge of Villanie', in 1598.

'Histriomastix' regarded as his first play was produced 1599. It's performance kicked off an episode in literary history known as the War of the Theatres; a literary feud between Marston, Jonson and Dekker that lasted until 1602.

However, the playwrights were later reconciled; Marston wrote a prefatory poem for Jonson's 'Sejanus' in 1605 and dedicated 'The Malcontent' to him.

Beyond this episode Marston's career continued to gather both strength, assets and followers. In 1603, he became a shareholder in the Children of Blackfriars company. He wrote and produced two plays with the company. The first was 'The Malcontent' in 1603, his most famous play. His second was 'The Dutch Courtesan', a satire on lust and hypocrisy, in 1604-5.

In 1605, he worked with George Chapman and Ben Jonson on 'Eastward Ho', a satire of popular taste and the vain imaginings of wealth to be found in the colony of Virginia.

Marston took the theatre world by surprise when he gave up writing plays in 1609 at the age of thirty-three. He sold his shares in the company of Blackfriars. His departure from the literary scene may have been because of further offence he gave to the king. The king suspended performances at Blackfriars and had Marston imprisoned.

On 24th September 1609 he was made a deacon and them a priest on 24th December 1609. In October 1616, Marston was assigned the living of Christchurch, Hampshire.

He died (accounts vary) on either the 24th or 25th June 1634 in London and was buried in the Middle Temple Church.

Index of Contents

TO THE WORLD'S MIGHTY MONARCH, GOOD OPINION

Sole regent of affection, perpetual ruler of judgment, most famous justice of censures, only giver of honour, great procurer of advancement, the world's chief balance, the all of all, and all in all, by whom all things are that that they are, I humbly offer this my poem.

Thou soul of pleasure, honour's only substance,
Great arbitrator, umpire of the earth,
Whom fleshly epicures call virtue's essence;
Thou moving orator, whose powerful breath
Sways all men's judgment—Great Opinion,

Vouchsafe to gild my imperfection.
If thou but deign to grace my blushing style,
And crown my muse with good opinion;
If thou vouchsafe with gracious eye to smile
Upon my young new-born invention,
I'll sing a hymn in honour of thy name
And add some trophy to enlarge thy fame.
But if thou wilt not with thy deity
Shade and inmask the errors of my pen,
Protect an orphan poet's infancy,
I will disclose, that all the world shall ken
How partial thou art in honours giving,
Crowning the shade, the substance' praise depriving.
W. K

.

THE ARGUMENT OF THE POEM

Pygmalion, whose chaste mind all the beauties in Cyprus could not ensnare, yet, at the length having carved in ivory an excellent proportion of a beauteous woman, was so deeply enamoured on his own workmanship that he would oftentimes lay the image in bed with him, and fondly use such petitions and dalliance as if it had been a breathing creature. But in the end, finding his fond dotage, and yet persevering in his ardent affection, made his devout prayers to Venus, that she would vouchsafe to inspire life into his love, and then join them both together in marriage. Whereupon Venus, graciously condescending to his earnest suit, the maid (by the power of her deity) was metamorphosed into a living woman. And after, Pygmalion (being in Cyprus) begat a son of her, which was called Paphus; whereupon that island Cyprus, in honour of Venus, was after, and is now, called by the inhabitants, Paphos.

TO HIS MISTRESS

My wanton muse lasciviously doth sing
Of sportive love, of lovely dallying.
O beauteous angel! deign thou to infuse
A sprightly wit into my dullèd muse.
I invoke none other saint but thee,
To grace the first blooms of my poesy.
Thy favours, like Promethean sacred fire,
In dead and dull conceit can life inspire;
Or, like that rare and rich elixir stone,
Can turn to gold leaden invention.
Be gracious then, and deign to show in me
The mighty power of thy deity;
And as thou read'st (fair) take compassion—
Force me not envy my Pygmalion:
Then when thy kindness grants me such sweet bliss,

I'll gladly write thy Metamorphosis.

PYGMALION

Pygmalion, whose high love-hating mind
Disdain'd to yield servile affection
Or amorous suit to any woman-kind,
Knowing their wants and men's perfection;
Yet love at length forced him to know his fate,
And love the shade whose substance he did hate.

For having wrought in purest ivory
So fair an image of a woman's feature,
That never yet proudest mortality
Could show so rare and beauteous a creature
(Unless my mistress' all-excelling face,
Which gives to beauty beauty's only grace)—

He was amazèd at the wondrous rareness
Of his own workmanship's perfection.
He thought that Nature ne'er produced such fairness,
In which all beauties have their mansion;
And, thus admiring, was enamourèd
On that fair image himself portrayèd.

And naked as it stood before his eyes,
Imperious Love declares his deity:
O what alluring beauties he descries
In each part of his fair imagery!
Her nakedness each beauteous shape contains;
All beauty in her nakedness remains.

He thought he saw the blood run through the vein
And leap, and swell with all alluring means;
Then fears he is deceived, and then again
He thinks he seeth the brightness of the beams
Which shoot from out the fairness of her eye;
At which he stands as in an ecstasy.

Her amber-colourèd, her shining hair,
Makes him protest the sun hath spread her head
With golden beams, to make her far more fair;
But when her cheeks his amorous thoughts have fed,
Then he exclaims, "Such red and so pure white,
Did never bless the eye of mortal sight!"

Then views her lips, no lips did seem so fair
In his conceit, through which he thinks doth fly
So sweet a breath, that doth perfume the air;
Then next her dimpled chin he doth descry,
And views and wonders, and yet views her still,—
Love's eyes in viewing never have their fill.

Her breasts like polish'd ivory appear,
Whose modest mount do bless admiring eye,
And makes him wish for such a pillowbear.
Thus fond Pygmalion striveth to descry
Each beauteous part, not letting over-slip
One parcel of his curious workmanship;

Until his eye descended so far down
That it descrièd Love's pavilion,
Where Cupid doth enjoy his only crown,
And Venus hath her chiefest mansion:
There would he wink, and winking look again,
Both eyes and thoughts would gladly there remain.

Who ever saw the subtile city-dame
In sacred church, when her pure thoughts should pray,
Peer through her fingers, so to hide her shame,
When that her eye, her mind would fain bewray:
So would he view and wink, and view again;
A chaster thought could not his eyes retain.

He wondered that she blush'd not when his eye
Saluted those same parts of secresy:
Conceiting not it was imagery
That kindly yielded that large liberty.
O that my mistress were an image too,
That I might blameless her perfections view!

But when the fair proportion of her thigh
Began appear, "O Ovid!" would he cry,
"Did e'en Corinna show such ivory
When she appeared in Venus livery!"
And thus enamour'd dotes on his own art
Which he did work, to work his pleasing smart.

And fondly doting, oft he kiss'd her lip;
Oft would he dally with her ivory breasts;
No wanton love-trick would he over-slip,
But still observ'd all amorous beheasts,
Whereby he thought he might procure the love
Of his dull image, which no plaints could move.

Look how the peevish Papists crouch and kneel
To some dumb idol with their offering,
As if a senseless carvèd stone could feel
The ardour of his bootless chattering,
So fond he was, and earnest in his suit
To his remorseless image, dumb and mute.

He oft doth wish his soul might part in sunder
So that one half in her had residence;
Oft he exclaims, "O beauty's only wonder!
Sweet model of delight, fair excellence,
Be gracious unto him that formèd thee,
Compassionate his true love's ardency."

She with her silence seems to grant his suit;
Then he all jocund, like a wanton lover,
With amorous embracements doth salute
Her slender waist, presuming to discover
The vale of Love, where Cupid doth delight
To sport and dally all the sable night.

His eyes her eyes kindly encounterèd;
His breast her breast oft joinèd close unto;
His arms' embracements oft she sufferèd;
Hands, arms, eyes, tongue, lips, and all parts did woo;
His thigh with hers, his knee play'd with her knee,—
A happy consort when all parts agree!

But when he saw, poor soul, he was deceivèd
(Yet scarce he could believe his sense had failed),
Yet when he found all hope from him bereavèd,
And saw how fondly all his thoughts had erred,
Then did he like to poor Ixion seem,
That clipt a cloud instead of Heaven's Queen.

I oft have smiled to see the foolery
Of some sweet youths, who seriously protest
That love respects not actual luxury,
But only joys to dally, sport, and jest;
Love is a child, contented with a toy;
A busk-point or some favour stills the boy.

Mark my Pygmalion, whose affections' ardour
May be a mirror to posterity;
Yet viewing, touching, kissing (common favour),
Could never satiate his love's ardency:
And therefore, ladies, think that they ne'er love you,

Who do not unto more than kissing move you.

For Pygmalion kiss'd, view'd, and embraced,
And yet exclaims, "Why were these women made,
O sacred gods, and with such beauties graced!
Have they not power as well to cool and shade,
As for to heat men's hearts? Or is there none,
Or are they all, like mine, relentless stone?"

With that he takes her in his loving arms,
And down within a down-bed softly laid her;
Then on his knees he all his senses charms,
To invocate sweet Venus for to raise her
To wishèd life, and to infuse some breath
To that which, dead, yet gave a life to death.

"Thou sacred queen of sportive dallying"
(Thus he begins), "Love's only emperess,
Whose kingdom rests in wanton revelling,
Let me beseech thee show thy powerfulness
In changing stone to flesh! Make her relent,
And kindly yield to thy sweet blandishment.

"O gracious goodess, take compassion;
Instil into her some celestial fire,
That she may equalise affection,
And have a mutual love, and love's desire!
Thou know'st the force of love, then pity me—
Compassionate my true love's ardency."

Thus having said, he riseth from the floor
As if his soul divinèd him good fortune,
Hoping his prayers to pity moved some power;
For all his thoughts did all good luck importune;
And therefore straight he strips him naked quite,
That in the bed he might have more delight.

Then thus, "Sweet sheets," he says, "which now do cover
The idol of my soul, the fairest one
That ever loved, or had an amorous lover—
Earth's only model of perfection—
Sweet happy sheets, deign for to take me in,
That I my hopes and longing thoughts may win!"

With that his nimble limbs do kiss the sheets,
And now he bows him for to lay him down;
And now each part with her fair parts do meet,
Now doth he hope for to enjoy love's crown;

Now do they dally, kiss, embrace together,
Like Leda's twins at sight of fairest weather.

Yet all's conceit—but shadow of that bliss
Which now my muse strives sweetly to display
In this my wondrous Metamorphosis.
Deign to believe me—now I sadly say—
The stony substance of his image feature
Was straight transform'd into a living creature!

For when his hands her fair-form'd limbs had felt,
And that his arms her naked waist embraced,
Each part like wax before the sun did melt,
And now, O now, he finds how he is graced
By his own work! Tut! women will relent
When as they find such moving blandishment.

Do but conceive a mother's passing gladness
(After that death her only son had seized,
And overwhelm'd her soul with endless sadness)
When that she sees him 'gin for to be raised
From out his deadly swoun to life again:
Such joy Pygmalion feels in every vein.

And yet he fears he doth but dreaming find
So rich content and such celestial bliss;
Yet when he proves and finds her wondrous kind,
Yielding soft touch for touch, sweet kiss for kiss,
He's well assured no fair imagery
Could yield such pleasing love's felicity.

O wonder not to hear me thus relate,
And say to flesh transformèd was a stone!
Had I my love in such a wishèd state
As was afforded to Pygmalion,
Though flinty-hard, of her you soon should see
As strange a transformation wrought by me.

And now methinks some wanton itching ear,
With lustful thoughts and ill attention,
Lists to my muse, expecting for to hear
The amorous description of that action
Which Venus seeks, and ever doth require,
When fitness grants a place to please desire.

Let him conceit but what himself would do
When that he had obtainèd such a favour
Of her to whom his thoughts were bound unto,

If she, in recompence of his love's labour,
Would deign to let one pair of sheets contain
The willing bodies of those loving twain.

Could he, O could he! when that each to either
Did yield kind kissing and more kind embracing—
Could he when that they felt and clipp'd together,
And might enjoy the life of dallying—
Could he abstain midst such a wanton sporting,
From doing that which is not fit reporting?

What would he do when that her softest skin
Saluted his with a delightful kiss;
When all things fit for love's sweet pleasuring
Invited him to reap a lover's bliss?
What he would do, the self-same action
Was not neglected by Pygmalion.

For when he found that life had took his seat
Within the breast of his kind beauteous love—
When that he found that warmth and wishèd heat
Which might a saint and coldest spirit move—
Then arms, eyes, hands, tongue, lips, and wanton thigh,
Were willing agents in love's luxury!

Who knows not what ensues? O pardon me!
Ye gaping ears that swallow up my lines,
Expect no more: peace, idle poesy,
Be not obscene though wanton in thy rhymes;
And, chaster thoughts, pardon if I do trip,
Or if some loose lines from my pen do slip.

Let this suffice, that that same happy night,
So gracious were the gods of marriage,
Midst all their pleasing and long-wish'd delight
Paphus was got; of whom in after age
Cyprus was Paphos call'd, and evermore
Those islanders do Venus' name adore.

The Author in Praise of His Precedent Poem

Now, Rufus, by old Glebron's fearful mace,
Hath not my muse deserved a worthy place?
Come, come, Luxurio, crown my head with bays,
Which, like a Paphian, wantonly displays
The Salaminian titillations,

Which tickle up our lewd Priapians.
Is not my pen complete? Are not my lines
Right in the swaggering humour of these times?
O sing pæana to my learnèd muse:
Io bis dicite! Wilt thou refuse?
Do not I put my mistress in before,
And piteously her gracious aid implore?
Do not I flatter, call her wondrous fair,
Virtuous, divine, most debonair?
Hath not my goddess, in the vaunt-guard place,
The leading of my lines their plumes to grace?
And then ensues my stanzas, like odd bands
Of voluntaries and mercenarians,
Which, like soldados of our warlike age,
March rich bedight in warlike equipage,
Glittering in dawbèd laced accoustrements,
And pleasing suits of love's habiliments;
Yet puffy as Dutch hose they are within,
Faint and white-liver'd, as our gallants bin;
Patch'd like a beggar's cloak, and run as sweet
As doth a tumbril in the pavèd street.
And in the end (the end of love, I wot),
Pygmalion hath a jolly boy begot.
So Labeo did complain his love was stone,
Obdurate, flinty, so relentless none;
Yet Lynceus knows that in the end of this
He wrought as strange a metamorphosis.
Ends not my poem then surpassing ill?
Come, come, Augustus, crown my laureate quill.

Now, by the whips of epigrammatists,
I'll not be lasht for my dissembling shifts;
And therefore I use Popelings' discipline,
Lay ope my faults to Mastigophoros' eyne;
Censure my self, 'fore others me deride
And scoff at me, as if I had denied
Or thought my poem good, when that I see
My lines are froth, my stanzas sapless be.
Thus having rail'd against myself a while,
I'll snarl at those which do the world beguile
With maskèd shows. Ye changing Proteans, list,
And tremble at a barking satirist.

SATIRES

SATIRE I

Quædam videntur, et non sunt.

I cannot show in strange proportion,
Changing my hue like a cameleon;
But you all-canning wits, hold water out,
Ye vizarded-bifronted-Janian rout.
Tell me, brown Ruscus, hast thou Gyges' ring,
That thou presumest as if thou wert unseen?
If not, why in thy wits half capreal
Lett'st thou a superscribèd letter fall?
And from thyself unto thyself dost send,
And in the same thyself thyself commend?
For shame! leave running to some satrapas,
Leave glavering on him in the peopled press;
Holding him on as he through Paul's doth walk,
With nods and legs and odd superfluous talk;
Making men think thee gracious in his sight,
When he esteems thee but a parasite.
For shame! unmask; leave for to cloke intent,
And show thou art vain-glorious, impudent.

Come, Briscus, by the soul of compliment,
I'll not endure that with thine instrument
(Thy gambo-viol placed betwixt thy thighs,
Wherein the best part of thy courtship lies)
Thou entertain the time, thy mistress by.
Come, now let's hear thy mounting Mercury.
What! mum? Give him his fiddle once again,
Or he's more mute than a Pythagoran.
But oh! the absolute Castilio,—
He that can all the points of courtship show;
He that can trot a courser, break a rush,
And arm'd in proof, dare dure a straw's strong push;
He, who on his glorious scutcheon
Can quaintly show wit's new invention,
Advancing forth some thirsty Tantalus,
Or else the vulture on Prometheus,
With some short motto of a dozen lines;
He that can purpose it in dainty rhymes,
Can set his face, and with his eye can speak,
Can dally with his mistress' dangling feak,
And wish that he were it, to kiss her eye
And flare about her beauty's deity:—
Tut! he is famous for his revelling,
For fine set speeches, and for sonnetting;
He scorns the viol and the scraping stick,
And yet's but broker of another's wit.

Certes, if all things were well known and view'd,
He doth but champ that which another chew'd.
Come, come, Castilion, skim thy posset curd,
Show thy queer substance, worthless, most absurd.
Take ceremonious compliment from thee!
Alas! I see Castilio's beggary.

O if Democritus were now alive,
How he would laugh to see this devil thrive!
And by an holy semblance blear men's eyes,
When he intends some damnèd villanies.
Ixion makes fair weather unto Jove,
That he might make foul work with his fair love;
And is right sober in his outward semblance,
Demure, and modest in his countenance;
Applies himself to great Saturnus' son,
Till Saturn's daughter yields his motion.
Night-shining Phœbe knows what was begat—
A monstrous Centaur illegitimate.

Who would not chuck to see such pleasing sport—
To see such troops of gallants still resort
Unto Cornuto's shop? What other cause
But chaste Brownetta, Sporo thither draws?
Who now so long hath praised the chough's white bill,
That he hath left her ne'er a flying quill:
His meaning gain, though outward semblance love,
So like a crabfish Sporo still doth move.
Laugh, laugh, to see the world, Democritus,
Cry like that strange transformèd Tereus.
Now Sorbo, with a feignèd gravity,
Doth fish for honour and high dignity.
Nothing within, nor yet without, but beard,
Which thrice he strokes, before I ever heard
One wise grave word to bless my listening ear.
But mark how Good Opinion doth him rear:
See, he's in office, on his foot-cloth placed;
Now each man caps, and strives for to be graced
With some rude nod of his majestic head,
Which all do wish in limbo harrièd.
But O I grieve that good men deign to be
Slaves unto him that's slave to villany!
Now Sorbo swells with self-conceited sense,
Thinking that men do yield this reverence
Unto his virtues: fond credulity!
Ass, take off Isis, no man honours thee.

Great Tubrio's feather gallantly doth wave,

Full twenty falls doth make him wondrous brave.
O golden jerkin! royal arming coat!
Like ship on sea, he on the land doth float.
He's gone, he's shipp'd, his resolution
Pricks him (by Heaven) to this action.
The pox it doth! Not long since did I view
The man betake him to a common stew;
And there (I wis), like no quaint-stomach'd man,
Eats up his arms; and war's munition,
His waving plume, falls in the broker's chest.
Fie! that his ostrich stomach should disgest
His ostrich feather, eat up Venice lace!
Thou that didst fear to eat poor-johns a space,
Lie close, ye slave, at beastly luxury!
Melt and consume in pleasure's surquedry!
But now, thou that didst march with Spanish pike before,
Come with French pox out of that brothel door.
The fleet's return'd. What news from Rodio?
"Hot service, by the Lord," cries Tubrio.
Why dost thou halt? "Why, six times through each thigh
Push'd with the pike of the hot enemy!
Hot service, hot, the Spaniard is a man;
I say no more, and as a gentleman
I served in his face. Farewell. Adieu."
Welcome from Netherland, from steaming stew.
Ass to thy crib, doff that huge lion's skin,
Or else the owl will hoot and drive thee in.
For shame, for shame! lewd-living Tubrio,
Presume not troop among that gallant crew
Of true heroic spirits; come, uncase,
Show us the true form of Dametas' face.
Hence, hence, ye slave! dissemble not thy state,
But henceforth be a turncoat, runagate.
O hold my sides! that I may break my spleen
With laughter at the shadows I have seen!

Yet I can bear with Curio's nimble feet,
Saluting me with capers in the street,
Although in open view and people's face,
He fronts me with some spruce, neat, cinquepace;
Or Tullus, though, whene'er he me espies,
Straight with loud mouth "A bandy, sir," he cries;
Or Robrus, who, addict to nimble fence,
Still greets me with stockado's violence.
These I do bear, because I too well know
They are the same they seem in outward show.
But all confusion sever from mine eye
This Janian bifront, Hypocrisy.

Quædam sunt, et non videntur.

I, that even now lisp'd like an amorist,
Am turn'd into a snaphance satirist.
O title, which my judgment doth adore!
But I, dull-sprited fat Bœotian boor,
Do far off honour that censorian seat;
But if I could in milk-white robes entreat
Plebeians' favour, I would show to be
Tribunus plebis, 'gainst the villany
Of these same Proteans, whose hypocrisy
Doth still abuse our fond credulity.
But since myself am not immaculate,
But many spots my mind doth vitiate,
I'll leave the white robe and the biting rhymes
Unto our modern Satire's sharpest lines,
Whose hungry fangs snarl at some secret sin,
And in such pitchy clouds enwrappèd been
His Sphinxian riddles, that old Œdipus
Would be amazed, and take it in foul snuffs
That such Cymmerian darkness should involve
A quaint conceit that he could not resolve.
O darkness palpable! Egypt's black night!
My wit is stricken blind, hath lost his sight;
My shins are broke with groping for some sense,
To know to what his words have reference.
Certes, sunt but non videntur that I know;
Reach me some poets' index that will show.
Imagines Deorum, Book of Epithets,
Natalis Comes, thou I know recites,
And makest anatomy of poesy;
Help me to unmask the satire's secrecy;
Delphic Apollo, aid me to unrip
These intricate deep oracles of wit—
These dark enigmas, and strange riddling sense,
Which pass my dullard brain's intelligence.
Fie on my senseless pate! Now I can show
Thou writest that which I nor thou dost know.
Who would imagine that such squint-eyed sight
Could strike the world's deformities so right?
But take heed, Pallas, lest thou aim awry;
Love nor yet Hate had e'er true-judging eye.
Who would once dream that that same elegy,

That fair-framed piece of sweetest poesy,
Which Muto put betwixt his mistress' paps
(When he, quick-witted, call'd her Cruel Chaps,
And told her there he might his dolors read
Which she, O she! upon his heart had spread),
Was penn'd by Roscio the tragedian?
Yet Muto, like a good Vulcanian—
An honest cuckold—calls the bastard, son,
And brags of that which others for him done.
Satire, thou liest, for that same elegy
Is Muto's own, his own dear poesy:
Why, 'tis his own, and dear, for he did pay
Ten crowns for it, as I heard Roscius say.—
Who would imagine yonder sober man,
That same devout meal-mouth'd precisian,
That cries "Good brother," "Kind sister," makes a duck
After the antique grace, can always pluck
A sacred book out of his civil hose,
And at th' op'ning and at our stomach's close,
Says with a turn'd-up eye a solemn grace
Of half an hour; then with silken face
Smiles on the holy crew, and then doth cry,
"O manners! O times of impurity!"
What that depaints a church-reformed state,
The which the female tongues magnificate,
Because that Plato's odd opinion
Of all things common hath strong motion
In their weak minds;—who thinks that this good man
Is a vile, sober, damned politician?
Not I, till with his bait of purity
He bit me sore in deepest usury.
No Jew, no Turk, would use a Christian
So inhumanely as this Puritan.
Diomedes' jades were not so bestial
As this same seeming saint—vile cannibal!
Take heed, O world! take heed advisedly
Of these same damnèd anthropophagi.
I had rather be within a harpy's claws
Than trust myself in their devouring jaws,
Who all confusion to the world would bring
Under the form of their new discipline.
O I could say, Briareus' hundred hands
Were not so ready to bring Jove in bands,
As these to set endless contentious strife
Betwixt Jehovah and his sacred wife!

But see—who's yonder? True Humility,
The perfect image of fair Courtesy;

See, he doth deign to be in servitude
Where he hath no promotion's livelihood!
Mark, he doth courtesy, and salutes a block,
Will seem to wonder at a weathercock;
Trenchmore with apes, play music to an owl,
Bless his sweet honour's running brasil bowl;
Cries "Bravely broke!" when that his lordship miss'd,
And is of all the throngèd scaffold hiss'd;
O is not this a courteous-minded man?
No fool, no; a damn'd Machiavelian;
Holds candle to the devil for a while,
That he the better may the world beguile,
That's fed with shows. He hopes, though some repine,
When sun is set the lesser stars will shine;
He is within a haughty malcontent,
Though he do use such humble blandishment.
But, bold-faced Satire, strain not over-high,
But laugh and chuck at meaner gullery.

In faith, yon is a well-faced gentleman;
See how he paceth like a Cyprian!
Fair amber tresses of the fairest hair
That ere were wavèd by our London air;
Rich lacèd suit, all spruce, all neat, in truth.
Ho, Lynceus! what's yonder brisk neat youth
'Bout whom yon troop of gallants flocken so,
And now together to Brown's Common go?
Thou know'st, I am sure; for thou canst cast thine eye
Through nine mud walls, or else old poets lie.
"'Tis loose-legg'd Lais, that same common drab
For whom good Tubrio took the mortal stab."
Ha, ha! Nay, then, I'll never rail at those
That wear a codpis, thereby to disclose
What sex they are, since strumpets breeches use,
And all men's eyes save Lynceus can abuse.
Nay, stead of shadow, lay the substance out,
Or else, fair Briscus, I shall stand in doubt
What sex thou art, since such hermaphrodites,
Such Protean shadows so delude our sights.

Look, look, with what a discontented grace
Bruto the traveller doth sadly pace
'Long Westminster! O civil-seeming shade,
Mark his sad colours!—how demurely clad!
Staidness itself, and Nestor's gravity,
Are but the shade of his civility.
And now he sighs: "O thou corrupted age,
Which slight regard'st men of sound carriage!

Virtue, knowledge, fly to heaven again;
Deign not 'mong these ungrateful sots remain!
Well, some tongues I know, some countries I have seen,
And yet these oily snails respectless been
Of my good parts." O worthless puffy slave!
Didst thou to Venice go ought else to have,
But buy a lute and use a courtesan,
And there to live like a Cyllenian?
And now from thence what hither dost thou bring,
But surphulings, new paints, and poisoning,
Aretine's pictures, some strange luxury,
And new-found use of Venice venery?
What art thou but black clothes? Sad Bruto, say,
Art anything but only sad array?
Which I am sure is all thou brought'st from France,
Save Naples pox and Frenchmen's dalliance;
From haughty Spain, what brought'st thou else beside
But lofty looks and their Lucifrian pride?
From Belgia, what but their deep bezeling,
Their boot-carouse and their beer-buttering?
Well, then, exclaim not on our age, good man,
But hence, polluted Neapolitan.

Now, Satire, cease to rub our gallèd skins,
And to unmask the world's detested sins;
Thou shalt as soon draw Nilus river dry
As cleanse the world from foul impiety.

SATIRE III

Quædam et sunt, et videntur.

Now, grim Reproof, swell in my rough-hued rhyme,
That thou mayst vex the guilty of our time.
Yon is a youth whom how can I o'er-slip,
Since he so jump doth in my meshes hit?
He hath been longer in preparing him
Than Terence wench; and now behold he's seen.
Now, after two years' fast and earnest prayer
The fashion change not (lest he should despair
Of ever hoarding up more fair gay clothes),
Behold at length in London street he shows.
His ruff did eat more time in neatest setting
Than Woodstock's work in painful perfecting;
It hath more doubles far than Ajax' shield
When he 'gainst Troy did furious battle wield.

Nay, he doth wear an emblem 'bout his neck;
For under that fair ruff so sprucely set,
Appears a fall, a falling-band forsooth.
O dapper, rare, complete, sweet nitty youth!
Jesu Maria! How his clothes appear
Cross'd and recross'd with lace, sure for some fear
Lest that some spirit with a tippet mace
Should with a ghastly show affright his face.
His hat, himself, small crown and huge great brim,
Fair outward show, and little wit within.
And all the band with feathers he doth fill,
Which is a sign of a fantastic still.
Why, so he is, his clothes do sympathise
And with his inward spirit humorise,
As sure as (some do tell me) evermore
A goat doth stand before a brothel door.
His clothes perfumed, his fusty mouth is aired,
His chin new swept, his very cheeks are glaired.

But ho! what Ganymede is that doth grace
The gallant's heels? One who for two days' space
Is closely hired. Now who dares not call
This Æsop's crow—fond, mad, fantastical?
An open ass, that is not yet so wise
As his derided fondness to disguise.
Why, thou art Bedlam mad, stark lunatic,
And glori'st to be counted a fantastic;
Thou neither art, nor yet will seem to be,
Heir to some virtuous praisèd quality.
O frantic man! that thinks all villany
The complete honours of nobility!
When some damn'd vice, some strange misshapen suit,
Make youths esteem themselves in high repute.
O age! in which our gallants boast to be
Slaves unto riot and rude luxury!
Nay, when they blush, and think an honest act
Doth their supposèd virtues maculate!
Bedlam, Frenzy, Madness, Lunacy,
I challenge all your moody empery
Once to produce a more distracted man
Than is inamorato Lucian.
For when my ears received a fearful sound
That he was sick, I went, and there I found
Him laid of love, and newly brought to bed
Of monstrous folly and a frantic head.
His chamber hang'd about with elegies,
With sad complaints of his love's miseries;
His windows strew'd with sonnets, and the glass

Drawn full of love-knots. I approach'd the ass,
And straight he weeps, and sighs some sonnet out
To his fair love! And then he goes about
For to perfume her rare perfection
With some sweet-smelling pink epitheton;
Then with a melting look he writhes his head,
And straight in passion riseth in his bed;
And having kiss'd his hand, stroke up his hair,
Made a French conge, cries, "O cruel fear!"
To the antic bedpost. I laugh'd amain,
That down my cheeks the mirthful drops did rain.
Well, he's no Janus, but substantial,
In show and essence a good natural;
When as thou hear'st me ask spruce Duceus
From whence he comes; and he straight answers us,
From Lady Lilla; and is going straight
To the Countess of (—), for she doth wait
His coming, and will surely send her coach,
Unless he make the speedier approach:
Art not thou ready for to break thy spleen
At laughing at the fondness thou hast seen
In this vain-glorious fool, when thou dost know
He never durst unto these ladies show
His pippin face? Well, he's no accident,
But real, real, shameless, impudent;
And yet he boasts, and wonders that each man
Can call him by his name, sweet Ducean;
And is right proud that thus his name is known.
Ay, Duceus, ay, thy name is too far blown:
The world too much, thyself too little know'st,
Thy private self. Why, then, should Duceus boast?
But, humble Satire, wilt thou deign display
These open nags, which purblind eyes bewray?
Come, come, and snarl more dark at secret sin,
Which in such labyrinths enwrappèd bin,
That, Ariadne, I must crave thy aid
To help me find where this foul monster's laid;
Then will I drive the Minotaur from us,
And seem to be a second Theseus.

SATIRE IV

Reactio.

Now doth Rhamnusia Adrastian,
Daughter of Night, and of the Ocean,

Provoke my pen. What cold Saturnian
Can hold, and hear such vile detraction?
Ye pines of Ida, shake your fair-grown height,
For Jove at first dash will with thunder fight;
Ye cedars, bend, 'fore lightning you dismay;
Ye lions tremble, for an ass doth bray.
Who cannot rail?—what dog but dare to bark
'Gainst Phœbe's brightness in the silent dark?
What stinking scavenger (if so he will,
Though streets be fair) but may right easily fill
His dungy tumbrel? Sweep, pare, wash, make clean,
Yet from your fairness he some dirt can glean.
The windy-colic striv'd to have some vent,
And now 'tis flown, and now his rage is spent.
So have I seen the fuming waves to fret,
And in the end naught but white foam beget;
So have I seen the sullen clouds to cry,
And weep for anger that the earth was dry,
After their spite that all the hail-shot drops
Could never pierce the crystal water tops,
And never yet could work her more disgrace
But only bubble quiet Thetis' face
Vain envious detractor from the good,
What cynic spirit rageth in thy blood?
Cannot a poor mistaken title 'scape,
But thou must that into thy tumbrel scrape?
Cannot some lewd immodest beastliness
Lurk and lie hid in just forgetfulness,
But Grillus' subtile-smelling swinish snout
Must scent and grunt, and needs will find it out?
Come, dance, ye stumbling satyrs by his side,
If he list once the Sion Muse deride;
Ye Granta's white nymphs, come, and with you bring
Some sillabub, whilst he doth sweetly sing
'Gainst Peter's tears and Mary's moving moan,
And like a fierce enragèd boar doth foam
At sacred sonnets. O daring hardiment!
At Bartas' sweet Semains rail impudent;
At Hopkins, Sternhold, and the Scottish King,
At all translators that do strive to bring
That stranger language to our vulgar tongue,
Spit in thy poison their fair acts among;
Ding them all down from fair Jerusalem,
And mew them up in thy deserved Bedlam.

Shall Paynims honour their vile falsèd gods
With sprightly wits, and shall not we by odds
Far, far more strive with wit's best quintessence

To adore the sacred ever-living essence?
Hath not strong reason moved the legists' mind,
To say the fairest of all nature's kind
The prince by his prerogative may claim?
Why may not then our souls, without thy blame
(Which is the best thing that our God did frame),
Devote the best part to his sacred name,
And with due reverence and devotion,
Honour his name with our invention?
No, poesy not fit for such an action,
It is defiled with superstition:
It honoured Baal, therefore pollute, pollute—
Unfit for such a sacred institute.
So have I heard a heretic maintain
The church unholy, where Jehovah's name
Is now adored, because he surely knows
Sometimes it was defiled with Popish shows;
The bells profane, and not to be endured,
Because to Popish rites they were inured.
Pure madness! Peace, cease to be insolent,
And be not outward sober, inly impudent.
Fie, inconsiderate! it grieveth me
An academic should so senseless be.
Fond censurer! why should those mirrors seem
So vile to thee, which better judgments deem
Exquisite then, and in our polish'd times
May run for senseful tolerable lines?
What, not mediocria firma from thy spite?
But must thy envious hungry fangs needs light
On Magistrates' Mirror? Must thou needs detract
And strive to work his ancient honour's wrack?
What, shall not Rosamond or Gaveston
Ope their sweet lips without detraction?
But must our modern critic's envious eye
Seem thus to quote some gross deformity,
Where art, not error, shineth in their style,
But error, and no art, doth thee beguile?
For tell me, critic, is not fiction
The soul of poesy's invention?
Is't not the form, the spirit, and the essence,
The life, and the essential difference,
Which omni, semper, soli, doth agree
To heavenly descended poesy?
Thy wit God comfort, mad chirurgion.
What, make so dangerous an incision?—
At first dash whip away the instrument
Of poet's procreation! Fie, ignorant!
When as the soul and vital blood doth rest,

And hath in fiction only interest,
What, Satire, suck the soul from poesy,
And leave him spriteless! O impiety!
Would ever any erudite pedant
Seem in his artless lines so insolent?
But thus it is when petty Priscians
Will needs step up to be censorians.
When once they can in true scann'd verses frame
A brave encomium of good Virtue's name;
Why, thus it is, when mimic apes will strive
With iron wedge the trunks of oaks to rive.

But see, his spirit of detraction
Must nibble at a glorious action.
Euge! some gallant spirit, some resolvèd blood,
Will hazard all to work his country's good,
And to enrich his soul and raise his name,
Will boldly sail unto the rich Guiane:
What then? Must straight some shameless satirist,
With odious and opprobrious terms insist
To blast so high resolv'd intention
With a malignant vile detraction?
So have I seen a cur dog in the street
Piss 'gainst the fairest posts he still could meet;
So have I seen the March wind strive to fade
The fairest hue that art or nature made:
So envy still doth bark at clearest shine,
And strives to stain heroic acts divine.
Well, I have cast thy water, and I see
Th' art fall'n to wit's extremest poverty,
Sure in consumption of the spritely part.
Go, use some cordial for to cheer thy heart,
Or else I fear that I one day shall see
Thee fall into some dangerous lethargy.

But come, fond braggart, crown thy brows with bay,
Intrance thyself in thy sweet ecstasy;
Come, manumit thy plumy pinion,
And scour the sword of elvish champion;
Or else vouchsafe to breathe in wax-bound quill,
And deign our longing ears with music fill;
Or let us see thee some such stanzas frame,
That thou mayst raise thy vile inglorious name.
Summon the Nymphs and Dryades to bring
Some rare invention, whilst thou dost sing
So sweet that thou mayst shoulder from above
The eagle from the stairs of friendly Jove,
And lead sad Pluto captive with thy song,

Gracing thyself, that art obscured so long.
Come, somewhat say (but hang me when 'tis done)
Worthy of brass and hoary marble stone;
Speak, ye attentive swains, that heard him never,
Will not his pastorals endure for ever?
Speak, ye that never heard him ought but rail,
Do not his poems bear a glorious sail?
Hath not he strongly justled from above
The eagle from the stairs of friendly Jove?
May be, may be; tut! 'tis his modesty;
He could, if that he would: nay, would, if could, I see.
Who cannot rail, and with a blasting breath
Scorch even the whitest lilies of the earth?
Who cannot stumble in a stuttering style,
And shallow heads with seeming shades beguile?
Cease, cease, at length to be malevolent
To fairest blooms of virtues eminent;
Strive not to soil the freshest hues on earth
With thy malicious and upbraiding breath.
Envy, let pines of Ida rest alone,
For they will grow spite of thy thunder-stone;
Strive not to nibble in their swelling grain
With toothless gums of thy detracting brain;
Eat not thy dam, but laugh and sport with me
At strangers' follies with a merry glee.
Let's not malign our kin. Then, satirist,
I do salute thee with an open fist.

SATIRE V

Parva magna, magna nulla.

Ambitious Gorgons, wide-mouth'd Lamians,
Shape-changing Proteans, damn'd Briarians,
Is Minos dead, is Rhadamanth asleep,
That ye thus dare unto Jove's palace creep?
What, hath Rhamnusia spent her knotted whip,
That ye dare strive on Hebe's cup to sip?
Yet know Apollo's quiver is not spent,
But can abate your daring hardiment.
Python is slain, yet his accursèd race
Dare look divine Astrea in the face;
Chaos return, and with confusion
Involve the world with strange disunion;
For Pluto sits in that adorèd chair
Which doth belong unto Minerva's heir.

O hecatombe! O catastrophe!
From Midas' pomp to Irus' beggary!
Prometheus, who celestial fire
Did steal from heaven, therewith to inspire
Our earthly bodies with a senseful mind,
Whereby we might the depth of nature find,
Is ding'd to hell, and vulture eats his heart,
Which did such deep philosophy impart
To mortal men; when thieving Mercury,
That even in his new-born infancy
Stole fair Apollo's quiver and Jove's mace,
And would have filch'd the lightning from his place,
But that he fear'd he should have burnt his wing
And sing'd his downy feathers' new-come spring;
He that in ghastly shade of night doth lead
Our souls unto the empire of the dead;
When he that better doth deserve a rope
Is a fair planet in our horoscope,
And now hath Caduceus in his hand,
Of life and death that hath the sole command.
Thus petty thefts are paid and soundly whipt,
But greater crimes are slightly overslipt;
Nay, he's a god that can do villany
With a good grace and glib facility.

The harmless hunter, with a ventrous eye,
When unawares he did Diana spy
Nak'd in the fountain, he became straightway
Unto his greedy hounds a wishèd prey,
His own delights taking away his breath,
And all ungrateful forced his fatal death
(And ever since hounds eat their masters clean,
For so Diana curst them in the stream).
When strong-back'd Hercules, in one poor night,
With great, great ease, and wonderous delight,
In strength of lust and Venus' surquedry,
Robb'd fifty wenches of virginity—
Far more than lusty Laurence—yet, poor soul,
He with Actæon drinks of Nemis' bowl:
When Hercules' lewd act is registered,
And for his fruitful labour deified,
And had a place in heaven him assigned,
When he the world unto the world resigned.
Thus little scapes are deeply punishèd,
But mighty villains are for gods adored.
Jove brought his sister to a nuptial bed,
And hath an Hebe and a Ganymede,
A Leda, and a thousand more beside

His chaste Alcmena and his sister-bride,
Who 'fore his face was odiously defil'd,
And by Ixion grossly got with child:
This thunderer, that right vertuously
Thrust forth his father from his empery,
Is now the great monarcho of the earth,
Whose awful nod, whose all-commanding breath,
Shakes Europe's ground-work; and his title makes
As dread a noise as when a cannon shakes
The subtile air. Thus hell-bred villany
Is still rewarded with high dignity,
When Sisyphus, that did but once reveal
That this incestuous villain had to deal
In isle Phliunte with Ægina fair,
Is damn'd to hell, in endless black despair
Ever to rear his tumbling stone upright
Upon the steepy mountain's lofty height;
His stone will never now get greenish moss,
Since he hath thus incurred so great a loss
As Jove's high favour. But it needs must be
Whilst Jove doth rule and sway the empery.
And poor Astrea's fled into an isle,
And lives a poor and banishèd exile,
And there penn'd up, sighs in her sad lament,
Wearing away in pining languishment.
If that Silenus' ass do chance to bray,
And so the satyrs' lewdness doth bewray,
Let him for ever be a sacrifice;
Prick, spur, beat, load, for ever tyrannise
Over the fool. But let some Cerberus
Keep back the wife of sweet-tongued Orpheus,
Gnato applauds the hound. Let that same child
Of night and sleep (which hath the world defiled
With odious railing) bark 'gainst all the work
Of all the gods, and find some error lurk
In all the graces; let his laver lip
Speak in reproach of Nature's workmanship;
Let him upbraid fair Venus, if he list,
For her short heel; let him with rage insist
To snarl at Vulcan's man, because he was
Not made with windows of transparent glass,
That all might see the passions of his mind;
Let his all-blasting tongue great errors find
In Pallas' house, because if next should burn,
It could not from the sudden peril turn;
Let him upbraid great Jove with luxury,
Condemn the heaven's queen of jealousy:
Yet this same Stygian Momus must be praised,

And to some godhead at the least be raised.
But if poor Orpheus sing melodiously,
And strive with music's sweetest symphony
To praise the gods, and unadvisedly
Do but o'er-slip one drunken deity,
Forthwith the bouzing Bacchus out doth send
His furious Bacchides, to be revenged;
And straight they tear the sweet musician,
And leave him to the dogs' division.
Hebrus, bear witness of their cruelty,
For thou didst view poor Orpheus' tragedy.
Thus slight neglects are deepest villany,
But blasting mouths deserve a deity.
Since Gallus slept, when he was set to watch
Lest Sol or Vulcan should Mavortius catch
In using Venus; since the boy did nap,
Whereby bright Phœbus did great Mars intrap,
Poor Gallus now (whilom to Mars so dear)
Is turnèd to a crowing chaunticlere;
And ever since, 'fore that the sun doth shine
(Lest Phœbus should with his all-piercing eyne
Descry some Vulcan), he doth crow full shrill,
That all the air with echoes he doth fill;
Whilst Mars, though all the gods do see his sin,
And know in what lewd vice he liveth in,
Yet is adored still, and magnified,
And with all honours duly worshipped.
Euge! Small faults to mountains straight are raised;
Slight scapes are whipt, but damnèd deeds are praised.

Fie, fie! I am deceived all this while,
A mist of errors doth my sense beguile;
I have been long of all my wits bereaven;
Heaven for hell taking, taking hell for heaven;
Virtue for vice, and vice for virtue still;
Sour for sweet, and good for passing ill.
If not, would vice and odious villany
Be still rewarded with high dignity?
Would damned Jovians be of all men praised,
And with high honours unto heaven raised?

'Tis so, 'tis so; riot and luxury
Are virtuous, meritorious chastity:
That which I thought to be damn'd hell-born pride,
Is humble modesty, and nought beside;
That which I deemèd Bacchus' surquedry,
Is grave and staid, civil sobriety.
O then, thrice holy age, thrice sacred men,

'Mong whom no vice a satire can discern,
Since lust is turnèd into chastity,
And riot unto sad sobriety,
Nothing but goodness reigneth in our age,
And virtues all are join'd in marriage!
Here is no dwelling for impiety,
No habitation for base villany;
Here are no subject for reproof's sharp vein;
Then hence, rude satire, make away amain,
And seek a seat where more impurity
Doth lie and lurk in still security!

Now doth my satire stagger in a doubt,
Whether to cease or else to write it out.
The subject is too sharp for my dull quill;
Some son of Maia, show thy riper skill;
For I'll go turn my tub against the sun,
And wistly mark how higher planets run,
Contemplating their hidden motion.
Then on some Latmos with Endymion,
I'll slumber out my time in discontent,
And never wake to be malevolent,
A beadle to the world's impurity.
But ever sleep in still security.
If this displease the world's wrong-judging sight,
It glads my soul, and in some better sprite
I'll write again. But if that this do please,
Hence, hence, satiric Muse, take endless ease,
Hush now, ye band-dogs, bark no more at me,
But let me slide away in secrecy.

THE SCOURGE OF VILLAINY

To Detraction I Present My Poesy

Foul canker of fair virtuous action,
Vile blaster of the freshest blooms on earth,
Envy's abhorrèd child, Detraction,
I here expose, to thy all-tainting breath,
The issue of my brain: snarl, rail, bark, bite,
Know that my spirit scorns Detraction's spite.

Know that the Genius, which attendeth on
And guides my powers intellectual,
Holds in all vile repute Detraction;
My soul an essence metaphysical,

That in the basest sort scorns critics' rage
Because he knows his sacred parentage.

My spirit is not puft up with fat fume
Of slimy ale, nor Bacchus' heating grape.
My mind disdains the dungy muddy scum
Of abject thoughts and Envy's raging hate.
True judgment slight regards Opinion,
A spritely wit disdains Detraction.

A partial praise shall never elevate
My settled censure of my own esteem;
A canker'd verdict of malignant hate
Shall ne'er provoke me worse myself to deem.
Spite of despite and rancour's villainy,
I am myself, so is my poesy.

In Lectores Prorsus Indignos

Fie, Satire, fie! shall each mechanic slave,
Each dunghill peasant, free perusal have
Of thy well-labour'd lines?—each satin suit,
Each quaint fashion-monger, whose sole repute
Rests in his trim gay clothes, lie slavering,
Tainting thy lines with his lewd censuring?
Shall each odd puisne of the lawyer's inn,
Each barmy-froth, that last day did begin
To read his little, or his ne'er a whit,
Or shall some greater ancient, of less wit
(That never turn'd but brown tobacco leaves,
Whose senses some damn'd occupant bereaves),
Lie gnawing on thy vacant time's expense,
Tearing thy rhymes, quite altering the sense?
Or shall perfum'd Castilio censure thee,
Shall he o'erview thy sharp-fang'd poesy
(Who ne'er read further than his mistress' lips),
Ne'er practised ought but some spruce cap'ring skips,
Ne'er in his life did other language use,
But "Sweet lady, fair mistress, kind heart, dear cuz"—
Shall this phantasma, this Coloss peruse,
And blast, with stinking breath, my budding muse?
Fie! wilt thou make thy wit a courtezan
For every broken handcraft's artisan?
Shall brainless cittern-heads, each jobbernoul,
Pocket the very genius of thy soul?

Ay, Phylo, ay, I'll keep an open hall,
A common and a sumptuous festival;
Welcome all eyes, all ears, all tongues to me,
Gnaw peasants on my scraps of poesy;
Castilios, Cyprians, court-boys, Spanish blocks,
Ribanded ears, Granado netherstocks,
Fiddlers, scriveners, pedlars, tinkering knaves,
Base blue-coats, tapsters, broad-cloth-minded slaves—
Welcome, i'faith; but may you ne'er depart
Till I have made your gallèd hides to smart.
Your gallèd hides? avaunt, base muddy scum,
Think you a satire's dreadful sounding drum
Will brace itself, and deign to terrify
Such abject peasants' basest roguery?
No, no, pass on, ye vain fantastic troop
Of puffy youths; know I do scorn to stoop
To rip your lives. Then hence, lewd nags, away,
Go read each post, view what is play'd to-day,
Then to Priapus' gardens. You, Castilio,
I pray thee let my lines in freedom go,
Let me alone, the madams call for thee,
Longing to laugh at thy wit's poverty.
Sirra livery cloak, you lazy slipper-slave,
Thou fawning drudge, what, wouldst thou satires have?
Base mind, away, thy master calls, be gone.
Sweet Gnato, let my poesy alone:
Go buy some ballad of the Fairy King,
And of the beggar wench some roguy thing,
Which thou mayst chant unto the chamber-maid
To some vile tune, when that thy master's laid.

But will you needs stay? am I forced to bear
The blasting breath of each lewd censurer?
Must naught but clothes, and images of men,
But spriteless trunks, be judges of thy pen?
Nay then, come all; I prostitute my muse,
For all the swarms of idiots to abuse.
Read all, view all; even with my full consent,
So you will know that which I never meant;
So you will ne'er conceive, and yet dispraise
That which you ne'er conceived, and laughter raise
Where I but strive in honest seriousness
To scourge some soul-polluting beastliness.
So you will rail, and find huge errors lurk
In every corner of my cynic work.
Proface, read on, for your extrem'st dislikes
Will add a pinion to my praise's flights.
O how I bristle up my plumes of pride,

O how I think my satire's dignifi'd,
When I once hear some quaint Castilio,
Some supple-mouth'd slave, some lewd Tubrio,
Some spruce pedant, or some span-new-come fry
Of inns-o'-court, striving to vilify
My dark reproofs! Then do but rail at me,
No greater honour craves my poesy.

I.
But, ye diviner wits, celestial souls,
Whose free-born minds no kennel-thought controlls,
Ye sacred spirits, Maia's eldest sons—

II.
Ye substance of the shadows of our age,
In whom all graces link in marriage,
To you how cheerfully my poem runs!

III.
True-judging eyes, quick-sighted censurers,
Heaven's best beauties, wisdom's treasurers,
O how my love embraceth your great worth!

IV.
Ye idols of my soul, ye blessed spirits,
How shall I give true honour to your merits,
Which I can better think than here paint forth!

You sacred spirits, Maia's eldest sons,
To you how cheerfully my poem runs!
O how my love embraceth your great worth,
Which I can better think than here paint forth!
O rare!

THE SCOURGE OF VILLAINY

PROEMIUM IN LIBRUM PRIMUM

I bear the scourge of just Rhamnusia,
Lashing the lewdness of Britannia.
Let others sing as their good genius moves,
Of deep designs, or else of clipping loves:
Fair fall them all, that with wit's industry
Do clothe good subjects in true poesy;
But as for me, my vexèd thoughtful soul
Takes pleasure in displeasing sharp control.

Thou nursing mother of fair Wisdom's lore,
Ingenuous Melancholy, I implore
Thy grave assistance: take thy gloomy seat,
Enthrone thee in my blood; let me entreat,
Stay his quick jocund skips, and force him run
A sad-paced course, until my whips be done.
Daphne, unclip thine arms from my sad brow;
Black cypress crown me, whilst I up do plow
The hidden entrails of rank villainy,
Tearing the veil from damn'd impiety.
Quake, guzzel dogs, that live on putrid slime,
Skud from the lashes of my yerking rhyme.

SATIRE I

Fronti nulla fides.

Marry, God forefend! Martius swears he'll stab:
Phrygio, fear not, thou art no lying drab.
What though dagger-hack'd mouths of his blade swears
It slew as many as figures of years
Aquafortis eat in't, or as many more
As methodist Musus kill'd with hellebore
In autumn last; yet he bears that male lie
With as smooth calm as Mecho rivalry.
How ill his shape with inward form doth fage,
Like Aphrogenia's ill-yoked marriage!
Fond physiognomer, complexion
Guides not the inward disposition,
Inclines I yield; thou sayst law; Julia,
Or Cato's often-curst Scatinia,
Can take no hold on simp'ring Lesbia.
True, not on her eye; yet alum oft doth blast
The sprouting bud that fain would longer last.
Chary Casca, right pure, or Rhodanus,
Yet each night drinks in glassy Priapus.

Yon pine is fair, yet foully doth it ill
To his own sprouts; mark, his rank drops distill
Foul Naples' canker in their tender rind.
Woe worth, when trees drop in their proper kind!
Mistagogus, what means this prodigy?
When Hiadolgo speaks 'gainst usury,
When Verres rails 'gainst thieves, Milo doth hate
Murder, Clodius cuckolds, Marius the gate

Of squinting Janus shuts? Run beyond bound
Of Nil ultra, and hang me when one's found
Will be himself. Had nature turn'd our eyes
Into our proper selves, these curious spies
Would be ashamed: Flavia would blush to flout
When Oppia calls Lucina help her out,
If she did think Lynceus did know her ill,
How nature art, how art doth nature spill.
God pardon me! I often did aver,
Quod gratis grate, the astronomer
An honest man; but I'll do so no more.
His face deceived me; but now, since his whore
And sister are all one, his honesty
Shall be as bare as his anatomy,
To which he bound his wife. O, packstaff rhymes!
Why not, when court of stars shall see these crimes?
Rods are in piss—ay, for thee, empirick,
That twenty grains of opium will not stick
To minister to babes. Here's bloody days,
When with plain herbs Mutius more men slays
Than ere third Edward's sword! Sooth, in our age,
Mad Coribantes need not to enrage
The people's minds. You, Ophiogeni
Of Hellespont, with wrangling villainy
The swoll'n world's inly stung, then deign a touch,
If that your fingers can effect so much.
Thou sweet Arabian Panchaia,
Perfume this nasty age: smug Lesbia
Hath stinking lungs, although a simp'ring grace,
A muddy inside, though a surphuled face.
O for some deep-searching Corycean,
To ferret out yon lewd Cinædian!

How now, Brutus, what shape best pleaseth thee?
All Protean forms, thy wife in venery,
At thy enforcement takes? Well, go thy way,
She may transform thee, ere thy dying day.
Hush, Gracchus hears, that hath retail'd more lies,
Broachèd more slanders, done more villainies,
Than Fabius' perpetual golden coat
(Which might have Semper idem for a mott)
Hath been at feasts, and led the measuring
At court, and in each marriage revelling;
Writ Palæphatus' comment on those dreams
That Hylus takes, 'midst dung-pit reeking steams
Of Athos' hot-house. Gramercy, modest smile,
Chremes asleep! Paphia, sport the while.
Lucia, new set thy ruff; tut, thou art pure,

Canst thou not lisp "good brother," look demure?
Fie, Gallus, what, a sceptic Pyrrhonist,
When chaste Dictynna breaks the zonelike twist?
Tut, hang up hieroglyphics. I'll not feign,
Wresting my humour from his native strain.

SATIRE II

Difficile est Satiram non scribere. —Juve.

I cannot hold, I cannot, I, endure
To view a big-womb'd foggy cloud immure
The radiant tresses of the quick'ning sun:
Let custards quake, my rage must freely run.
Preach not the Stoic's patience to me;
I hate no man, but men's impiety.
My soul is vex'd; what power will resist,
Or dares to stop a sharp-fang'd satirist?
Who'll cool my rage? who'll stay my itching fist?
But I will plague and torture whom I list.
If that the threefold walls of Babylon
Should hedge my tongue, yet I should rail upon
This fusty world, that now dare put in ure
To make JEHOVA but a coverture
To shade rank filth. Loose conscience is free
From all conscience, what else hath liberty?
As't please the Thracian Boreas to blow,
So turns our airy conscience to and fro.

What icy Saturnist, what northern pate,
But such gross lewdness would exasperate?
I think the blind doth see the flame-god rise
From sister's couch, each morning to the skies,
Glowing with lust. Walk but in dusky night
With Lynceus' eyes, and to thy piercing sight
Disguisèd gods will show, in peasants' shape,
Prest to commit some execrable rape.
Here Jove's lust-pander, Maia's juggling son,
In clown's disguise, doth after milkmaids run;
And, 'fore he'll lose his brutish lechery,
The trulls shall taste sweet nectar's surquedry.
There Juno's brat forsakes Neries' bed
And like a swaggerer, lust-firèd,
Attended only with his smock-sworn page,
Pert Gallus, slyly slips along, to wage
Tilting encounters with some spurious seed

Of marrow pies and yawning oysters' breed.
                    O damn'd!
Who would not shake a satire's knotty rod,
When to defile the sacred seat of God
Is but accounted gentlemen's disport?
To snort in filth, each hour to resort
To brothel-pits; alas! a venial crime,
Nay, royal, to be last in thirtieth slime!

Ay me! hard world for satirists begin
To set up shop, when no small petty sin
Is left unpurged! Once to be pursy fat,
Had wont because that life did macerate.
Marry, the jealous queen of air doth frown,
That Ganymede is up, and Hebe down.
Once Albion lived in such a cruel age
That men did hold by servile villenage:
Poor brats were slaves of bondmen that were born,
And marted, sold: but that rude law is torn
And disannull'd, as too too inhumane,
That lords o'er peasants should such service strain.
But now (sad changè!) the kennel sink of slaves,
Peasant great lords, and servile service craves.

Bond-slave sons had wont be bought and sold;
But now heroës' heirs (if they have not told
A discreet number 'fore their dad did die)
Are made much of: how much from merchandie?
Tail'd, and retail'd, till to the pedlar's pack
The fourth-hand ward-ware comes; alack, alack!
Would truth did know I lied: but truth and I
Do know that sense is born to misery.
Oh would to God this were their worst mischance,
Were not their souls sold to dark ignorance!
Fair godness is foul ill, if mischief's wit
Be not repress'd from lewd corrupting it.

O what dry brain melts not sharp mustard rhyme,
To purge the snottery of our slimy time!
Hence, idle "Cave," vengeance pricks me on,
When mart is made of fair religion.
Reform'd bald Trebus swore, in Romish quire,
He sold God's essence for a poor denier.
The Egyptians adorèd onions,
To garlic yielding all devotions.
O happy garlic, but thrice happy you,
Whose scenting gods in your large gardens grew!
Democritus, rise from thy putrid slime,

Sport at the madness of that hotter clime,
Deride their frenzy, that for policy
Adore wheat dough as real deity.
Almighty men, that can their Maker make,
And force his sacred body to forsake
The cherubins, to be gnawn actually,
Dividing individuum really;
Making a score of gods with one poor word.
Ay, so I thought, in that you could afford
So cheap a pennyworth. O ample field,
In which a satire may just weapon wield
But I am vex'd, when swarms of Julians
Are still manured by lewd precisians,
Who, scorning Church-rites, take the symbol up
As slovenly as careless courtiers slup
Their mutton gruel! Fie! who can withhold,
But must of force make his mild muse a scold,
When that he grievèd sees, with red vex'd eyes,
That Athens' ancient large immunities
Are eyesores to the Fates! Poor cells forlorn!
Is't not enough you are made an abject scorn
To jeering apes, but must the shadow too
Of ancient substance be thus wrung from you!
O split my heart, lest it do break with rage,
To see th' immodest looseness of our age!
Immodest looseness? fie, too gentle word,
When every sign can brothelry afford:
When lust doth sparkle from our females' eyes,
And modesty is roosted in the skies!

Tell me, Galliottæ, what means this sign,
When impropriate gentles will turn Capuchine?
Sooner be damn'd! O, stuff satirical!
When rapine feeds our pomp, pomp ripes our fall;
When the guest trembles at his host's swart look;
The son doth fear his stepdame, that hath took
His mother's place for lust; the twin-born brother
Maligns his mate, that first came from his mother;
When to be huge, is to be deadly sick;
When virtuous peasants will not spare to lick
The devil's tail for poor promotion;
When for neglect, slubber'd Devotion
Is wan with grief; when Rufus yawns for death
Of him that gave him undeservèd breath;
When Hermus makes a worthy question,
Whether of right, as paraphernalion,
A silver piss-pot fits his lady dame,
Or it's too good—a pewter best became;

When Agrippina poisons Claudius' son,
That all the world to her own brat might run;
When the husband gapes that his stale wife would die
That he might once be in by courtesy;
The big-paunch'd wife longs for her loath'd mate's death,
That she might have more jointures here on earth;
When tenure for short years (by many a one)
Is thought right good be turn'd forth Littleton,
All to be heady, or freehold at least,
When 'tis all one, for long life be a beast,
A slave, as have a short-term'd tenancy;
When dead's the strength of England's yeomanry;
When inundation of luxuriousness
Fats all the world with such gross beastliness:—
Who can abstain? What modest brain can hold,
But he must make his shame-faced muse a scold?

SATIRE III

Redde, age, quæ deinceps risisti.

It's good be wary, whilst the sun shines clear
(Quoth that old chuff that may dispend by year
Three thousand pound), whilst he of good pretence
Commits himself to Fleet, to save expense.
No country's Christmas—rather tarry here,
The Fleet is cheap, the country hall too dear.
But, Codrus, hark! the world expects to see
Thy bastard heir rot there in misery.
What! will Luxurio keep so great a hall
That he will prove a bastard in his fall?
No; "Come on five! St. George, by Heaven, at all!"
Makes his catastrophe right tragical!
At all? till nothing's left! Come on, till all comes off,
Ay, hair and all! Luxurio, left a scoff
To leprous filths! O stay, thou impious slave,
Tear not the lead from off thy father's grave
To stop base brokeage!—sell not thy father's sheet—
His leaden sheet, that strangers' eyes may greet
Both putrefaction of thy greedy sire
And thy abhorrèd viperous desire!
But wilt thou needs, shall thy dad's lacky brat
Wear thy sire's half-rot finger in his hat?
Nay, then, Luxurio, waste in obloquy,
And I shall sport to hear thee faintly cry,
"A die, a drab, and filthy broking knaves,

Are the world's wide mouths, all-devouring graves."
Yet Samus keeps a right good house, I hear—
No, it keeps him, and free'th him from chill fear
Of shaking fits. How, then, shall his smug wench,
How shall her bawd (fit time) assist her quench
Her sanguine heat? Lynceus, canst thou scent?
She hath her monkey and her instrument
Smooth fram'd at Vitrio. O grievous misery!
Luscus hath left his female luxury;
Ay, it left him! No, his old cynic dad
Hath forc'd him clean forsake his Pickhatch drab.
Alack, alack! what peace of lustful flesh
Hath Luscus left, his Priape to redress?
Grieve not, good soul, he hath his Ganymede,
His perfumed she-goat, smooth-kemb'd and high fed.
At Hogson now his monstrous love he feasts,
For there he keeps a bawdy-house of beasts.
Paphus, let Luscus have his courtezan,
Or we shall have a monster of a man.
Tut! Paphus now detains him from that bower,
And clasps him close within his brick-built tower.
Diogenes, thou art damn'd for thy lewd wit,
For Luscus now hath skill to practise it.
Faith, what cares he for fair Cinædian boys,
Velvet-caped goats, Dutch mares? Tut! common toys!
Detain them all on this condition,
He may but use his cynic friction.

O now, ye male stews, I can give pretence
For your luxurious incontinence.
Hence, hence, ye falsèd seeming patriots,
Return not with pretence of salving spots,
When here ye soil us with impurity,
And monstrous filth of Doway seminary.
What, though Iberia yield you liberty,
To snort in sauce of Sodom villainy?
What, though the blooms of young nobility,
Committed to your Rhodon's custody,
Ye, Nero-like, abuse? yet ne'er approach
Your new St. Omer's lewdness here to broach;
Tainting our towns and hopeful academes
With your lust-baiting, most abhorrèd means.

Valladolid, our Athens, 'gins to taste
Of thy rank filth. Camphire and lettuce chaste
Are clean cashier'd; now Sophi ringoes eat,
Candied potatoes are Athenians' meat.
Hence, holy thistle, come sweet marrow-pie,

Enflame our backs to itching luxury.
A crab's baked guts, a lobster's butter'd thigh,
I hear them swear is blood for venery.
Had I some snout-fair brats, they should endure
The new-found Castilion calenture
Before some pedant tutor, in his bed,
Should use my frie like Phrygian Ganymede.
Nay, then, chaste cells, when greasy Aretine,
For his rank fico, is surnamed divine;
Nay, then, come all ye venial scapes to me,
I dare well warrant you'll absolvèd be.
Rufus, I'll term thee but intemperate—
I will not once thy vice exaggerate—
Though that each hour thou lewdly swaggerest,
And at the quarter-day pay'st interest
For the forbearance of thy chalkèd score;
Though that thou keep'st a tally with thy whore:
Since Nero keeps his mother Agrippine,
And no strange lust can satiate Messaline.

Tullus, go scotfree; though thou often bragg'st
That, for a false French crown thou vaulting hadst;
Though that thou know'st, for thy incontinence,
Thy drab repaid thee true French pestilence.
But tush! his boast I bear, when Tegeran
Brags that he foists his rotten courtezan
Upon his heir, that must have all his lands,
And them hath join'd in Hymen's sacred bands.
I'll wink at Robrus, that for vicinage
Enters common on his next neighbour's stage;
When Jove maintains his sister and his whore,
And she incestuous, jealous evermore
Lest that Europa on the bull should ride;
Woe worth, when beasts for filth are deified!

Alack, poor rogues! what censor interdicts
The venial scapes of him that purses picks?
When some sly golden-slopp'd Castilio
Can cut a manor's strings at primero?
Or with a pawn shall give a lordship mate,
In statute-staple chaining fast his state?

What academic starved satirist
Would gnaw reez'd bacon, or, with ink-black fist,
Would toss each muck-heap for some outcast scraps
Of half-dung bones, to stop his yawning chaps?
Or, with a hungry, hollow, half-pined jaw
Would once a thrice-turn'd bone-pick'd subject gnaw,

When swarms of mountebanks and banditti,
Damn'd Briareans, sinks of villainy,
Factors for lewdness, brokers for the devil,
Infect our souls with all-polluting evil?

Shall Lucia scorn her husband's lukewarm bed
(Because her pleasure, being hurrièd
In jolting coach, with glassy instrument,
Doth far exceed the Paphian blandishment),
Whilst I (like to some mute Pythagoran)
Halter my hate, and cease to curse and ban
Such brutish filth? Shall Matho raise his fame
By printing pamphlets in another's name,
And in them praise himself, his wit, his might,
All to be deem'd his country's lanthorn-light?
Whilst my tongue's tied with bonds of blushing shame,
For fear of broaching my concealèd name?
Shall Balbus, the demure Athenian,
Dream of the death of next vicarian,
Cast his nativity, mark his complexion,
Weigh well his body's weak condition,
That, with gilt sleight, he may be sure to get
The planet's place when his dim shine shall set?
Shall Curio streak his limbs on his day's couch,
In summer bower, and with bare groping touch
Incense his lust, consuming all the year
In Cyprian dalliance, and in Belgic cheer?
Shall Faunus spend a hundred gallions
Of goat's pure milk to lave his stallions,
As much rose-juice? O bath! O royal, rich,
To scour Faunus and his salt-proud bitch.
And when all's cleans'd, shall the slave's inside stink
Worse than the new cast slime of Thames ebb'd brink,
Whilst I securely let him over-slip,
Ne'er yerking him with my satiric whip?

Shall Crispus with hypocrisy beguile,
Holding a candle to some fiend a while—
Now Jew, then Turk, then seeming Christian,
Then Atheist, Papist, and straight Puritan;
Now nothing, anything, even what you list,
So that some gilt may grease his greedy fist?

Shall Damas use his third-hand ward as ill
As any jade that tuggeth in the mill?
What, shall law, nature, virtue be rejected,
Shall these world-arteries be soul-infected
With corrupt blood, whilst I shall Martia task,

Or some young Villius all in choler ask
How he can keep a lazy waiting-man,
And buy a hood, and silver-handled fan,
With forty pound? Or snarl at Lollius' son,
That with industrious pains hath harder won
His true-got worship and his gentry's name
Than any swineherd's brat that lousy came
To luskish Athens and, with farming pots,
Compiling beds, and scouring greasy spots,
By chance (when he can, like taught parrot, cry
"Dearly belov'd," with simpering gravity)
Hath got the farm of some gelt vicary,
And now, on cock-horse, gallops jollily;
Tickling, with some stol'n stuff, his senseless cure,
Belching lewd terms 'gainst all sound literature?
Shall I with shadows fight, task bitterly
Rome's filth, scraping base channel roguery,
Whilst such huge giants shall affright our eyes
With execrable, damn'd inpieties?
Shall I find trading Mecho never loath
Frankly to take a damning perjured oath?
Shall Furia broke her sister's modesty,
And prostitute her soul to brothelry?
Shall Cossus make his well-faced wife a stale,
To yield his braided ware a quicker sale?
Shall cock-horse, fat-paunch'd Milo stain whole stocks
Of well-born souls with his adultering spots?
Shall broking panders suck nobility,
Soiling fair stems with foul impurity?
Nay, shall a trencher-slave extenuate
Some Lucrece rape, and straight magnificate
Lewd Jovian lust, whilst my satiric vein
Shall muzzled be, not daring out to strain
His tearing paw? No, gloomy Juvenal,
Though to thy fortunes I disastrous fall.

SATIRE IV

Cras.

Ay, marry, sir, here's perfect honesty,
When Martius will forswear all villainy
(All damn'd abuse of payment in the wars,
All filching from his prince and soldiers),
When once he can but so much bright dirt glean
As may maintain one more Whitefriars quean,

One drab more; faith, then farewell villainy,
He'll cleanse himself to Shoreditch purity.

As for Stadius, I think he hath a soul;
And if he were but free from sharp control
Of his sour host, and from his tailor's bill,
He would not thus abuse his rhyming skill;
Jading our tirèd ears with fooleries,
Greasing great slaves with oily flatteries.
Good faith, I think he would not strive to suit
The back of humorous Time (for base repute
'Mong dunghill peasants), botching up such ware
As may be saleable in Sturbridge fair,
If he were once but freed from specialty;
But sooth, till then, bear with his balladry.

I ask'd lewd Gallus when he'll cease to swear,
And with whole-culverin, raging oaths to tear
The vault of heaven—spitting in the eyes
Of Nature's nature loathsome blasphemies.
To-morrow, he doth vow, he will forbear.
Next day I meet him, but I hear him swear
Worse than before. I put his vow in mind.
He answers me "To-morrow;" but I find
He swears next day far worse than e'er before,
Putting me off with "morrow" evermore.
Thus, when I urge him, with his sophistry
He thinks to salve his damnèd perjury.

Silenus now is old, I wonder, I,
He doth not hate his triple venery.
Cold, writhled eld, his life-sweat almost spent,
Methinks a unity were competent.
But, O fair hopes! he whispers secretly,
When it leaves him he'll leave his lechery.

When simp'ring Flaccus (that demurely goes
Right neatly tripping on his new-black'd toes)
Hath made rich use of his religion,
Of God himself, in pure devotion;
When that the strange ideas in his head
(Broachèd 'mongst curious sots, by shadows led)
Have furnish'd him, by his hoar auditors,
Of fair demesnes and goodly rich manors;
Sooth, then, he will repent when's treasury
Shall force him to disclaim his heresy.
What will not poor need force? But being sped,
God for us all! the gurmond's paunch is fed;

His mind is changed. But when will he do good?
To-morrow,—ay, to-morrow, by the rood!

Yet Ruscus swears he'll cease to broke a suit,
By peasant means striving to get repute
'Mong puffy sponges, when the Fleet's defrayed,
His revel tire, and his laundress paid.
There is a crew which I too plain could name,
If so I might without th' Aquinians' blame,
That lick the tail of greatness with their lips—
Labouring with third-hand jests and apish skips,
Retailing others' wit, long barrellèd,
To glib some great man's ears till paunch be fed—
Glad if themselves, as sporting fools, be made
To get the shelter of some high-grown shade.
To-morrow yet these base tricks they'll cast off,
And cease for lucre be a jeering scoff.
Ruscus will leave when once he can renew
His wasted clothes, that are ashamed to view
The world's proud eyes; Drusus will cease to fawn
When that his farm, that leaks in melting pawn,
Some lord-applauded jest hath once set free:
All will to-morrow leave their roguery.
When fox-furr'd Mecho (by damn'd usury,
Cut-throat deceit, and his craft's villainy)
Hath raked together some four thousand pound,
To make his smug girl bear a bumming sound
In a young merchant's ear, faith, then (may be)
He'll ponder if there be a Deity;
Thinking, if to the parish poverty,
At his wish'd death, be doled a halfpenny,
A work of supererogation,
A good filth-cleansing strong purgation.

Aulus will leave begging monopolies
When that, 'mong troops of gaudy butterflies,
He is but able jet it jollily
In piebald suits of proud court bravery.

To-morrow doth Luxurio promise me
He will unline himself from bitchery;
Marry, Alcides thirteenth act must lend
A glorious period, and his lust-itch end,
When once he hath froth-foaming Ætna past,
At one-and-thirty, being always last.

If not to-day (quoth that Nasonian),
Much less to-morrow. "Yes," saith Fabian,

"For ingrain'd habits, dyed with often dips,
Are not so soon discolourèd. Young slips,
New set, are easily mov'd and pluck'd away;
But elder roots clip faster in the clay."
I smile at thee, and at the Stagyrite,
Who holds the liking of the appetite,
Being fed with actions often put in ure,
Hatcheth the soul in quality impure
Or pure; may be in virtue: but for vice,
That comes by inspiration, with a trice.
Young Furius, scarce fifteen years of age,
But is, straightways, right fit for marriage—
Unto the devil; for sure they would agree,
Betwixt their souls there is such sympathy.

O where's your sweaty habit, when each ape,
That can but spy the shadow of his shape,
That can no sooner ken what's virtuous,
But will avoid it, and be vicious!
Without much do or far-fetch'd habiture,
In earnest thus:—It is a sacred cure
To salve the soul's dread wounds; omnipotent
That Nature is, that cures the impotent,
Even in a moment. Sure, grace is infused
By Divine favour, not by actions used,
Which is as permanent as heaven's bliss,
To them that have it; then no habit is.
To-morrow, nay, to-day, it may be got,
So please that gracious power cleanse thy spot.
Vice, from privation of that sacred grace
Which God withdraws, but puts not vice in place.
Who says the sun is cause of ugly night?
Yet when he veils our eyes from his fair sight,
The gloomy curtain of the night is spread.
Ye curious sots, vainly by Nature led,
Where is your vice or virtuous habit now?
For Sustine pro nunc doth bend his brow,
And old crabb'd Scotus, on the Organon,
Pay'th me with snaphance, quick distinction.
"Habits, that intellectual termèd be,
Are got or else infused from Deity."
Dull Sorbonist, fly contradiction!
Fie! thou oppugn'st the definition;
If one should say, "Of things term'd rational,
Some reason have, others mere sensual,"
Would not some freshman, reading Porphyry,
Hiss and deride such blockish foolery?
"Then vice nor virtue have from habit place;

The one from want, the other sacred grace;
Infused, displaced; not in our will or force,
But as it please Jehovah have remorse."
I will, cries Zeno. O presumption!
I can. Thou mayst, doggèd opinion
Of thwarting cynics. To-day vicious;
List to their precepts, next day virtuous.
Peace, Seneca, thou belchest blasphemy!
"To live from God, but to live happily"
(I hear thee boast) "from thy philosophy,
And from thyself." O ravening lunacy!
Cynics, ye wound yourselves; for destiny,
Inevitable fate, necessity,
You hold, doth sway the acts spiritual,
As well as parts of that we mortal call.
Where's then I will? Where's that strong deity
You do ascribe to your philosophy?
Confounded Nature's brats! can will and fate
Have both their seat and office in your pate?
O hidden depth of that dread secrecy,
Which I do trembling touch in poetry!
To-day, to-day, implore obsequiously;
Trust not to-morrow's will, lest utterly
Ye be attach'd with sad confusion,
In your grace-tempting lewd presumption.

But I forget. Why sweat I out my brain
In deep designs to gay boys, lewd and vain?
These notes were better sung 'mong better sort;
But to my pamphlet, few, save fools, resort.

PROEMIUM IN LIBRUM SECUNDUM

I cannot quote a mott Italionate,
Or brand my satires with some Spanish term;
I cannot with swoll'n lines magnificate
Mine own poor worth, or as immaculate
Task others' rhymes, as if no blot did stain,
No blemish soil, my young satiric vein.

Nor can I make my soul a merchandise,
Seeking conceits to suit these artless times;
Or deign for base reward to poetise,
Soothing the world with oily flatteries.
Shall mercenary thoughts provoke me write—
Shall I for lucre be a parasite?

Shall I once pen for vulgar sorts applause,
To please each hound, each dungy scavenger;
To fit some oyster-wench's yawning jaws
With tricksey tales of speaking Cornish daws?
First let my brain (bright-hair'd Latona's son)
Be clean distract with all confusion.

What though some John-à-Stile will basely toil,
Only incited with the hope of gain:
Though roguey thoughts do force some jade-like moil;
Yet no such filth my true-born muse will soil.
O Epictetus, I do honour thee,
To think how rich thou wert in poverty!

Ad Rhythmum

Come, pretty pleasing symphony of words,
Ye well-match'd twins (whose like-tuned tongues affords
Such musical delight), come willingly
And dance lavoltas in my poesy.
Come all as easy as spruce Curio will,
In some court-hall, to show his cap'ring skill;
As willingly come, meet and jump together
As new-join'd loves, when they do clip each other;
As willingly as wenches trip around
About a May-pole after bagpipe's sound;
Come, rhyming numbers, come and grace conceit,
Adding a pleasing close, with your deceit
Enticing ears. Let not my ruder hand
Seem once to force you in my lines to stand;
Be not so fearful (pretty souls) to meet
As Flaccus is the sergeant's face to greet;
Be not so backward, loth to grace my sense,
As Drusus is to have intelligence
His dad's alive; but come into my head
As jocundly as (when his wife was dead)
Young Lælius to his home. Come, like-faced rhyme,
In tuneful numbers keeping music's time;
But if you hang an arse, like Tubered,
When Chremes dragg'd him from his brothel bed,
Then hence, base ballad-stuff, my poetry
Disclaims you quite; for know my liberty
Scorns rhyming laws. Alas, poor idle sound!
Since I first Phœbus knew I never found
Thy interest in sacred poesy;

Thou to invention add'st but surquedry,
A gaudy ornature, but hast no part
In that soul-pleasing high infusèd art.
Then if thou wilt clip kindly in my lines,
Welcome, thou friendly aid of my designs:
If not, no title of my senseless change
To wrest some forcèd rhyme, but freely range.
Ye scrupulous observers, go and learn
Of Æsop's dog; meat from a shade discern.

SATIRE V

Totum in toto.

Hang thyself, Drusus: hast nor arms nor brain?
So Sophi say, "The gods sell all for pain."
                                    Not so.
Had not that toiling Theban's steelèd back
Dread poisoned shafts, lived he now, he should lack
Spite of his farming ox-stalls. Themis' self
Would be cashier'd from one poor scrap of pelf.
If that she were incarnate in our time,
She might lusk, scornèd in disdainèd slime,
Shaded from honour by some envious mist
Of wat'ry fogs, that fill the ill-stuff'd list
Of fair Desert, jealous even of blind dark,
Lest it should spy, and at their lameness bark.
"Honour's shade thrusts honour's substance from his place."
'Tis strange, when shade the substance can disgrace.
"Harsh lines!" cries Curus, whose ears ne'er rejoice
But at the quavering of my lady's voice.
Rude limping lines fits this lewd halting age:
Sweet-scenting Curus, pardon then my rage,
When wisards swear plain virtue never thrives,
None but Priapus by plain dealing wives.
Then, subtile Hermes, are the destinies
Enamour'd on thee! Then up, mount the skies,
Advance, depose, do even what thou list,
So long as fates do grace thy juggling fist.
Tuscus, hast Beuclerc's arms and strong sinews,
Large reach, full-fed veins, ample revenues?
Then make thy markets by thy proper arm;
O brawny strength is an all-canning charm!
Thou dreadless Thracian! hast Hallirhothius slain?
What, is't not possible thy cause maintain
Before the dozen Areopagites?

Come, Enagonian, furnish him with sleights.
Tut, Pluto's wrath Proserpina can melt,
So that thy sacrifice be freely felt.
What! cannot Juno force in bed with Jove,
Turn and return a sentence with her love?—
Thou art too dusky.—Fie, thou shallow ass!
Put on more eyes, and mark me as I pass.
Well, plainly thus: "Sleight, force are mighty things,
From which much (if not most) earth's glory springs.
If virtue's self were clad in human shape,
Virtue without these might go beg and scrape.
The naked truth is, a well-clothèd lie,
A nimble quick pate mounts to dignity;
By force or fraud, that matters not a jot,
So massy wealth may fall unto thy lot."

I heard old Albius swear Flavus should have
His eldest girl, for Flavus was a knave,
A damn'd deep-reaching villain, and would mount
(He durst well warrant him) to great account;
What, though he laid forth all his stock and store
Upon some office, yet he'll gain much more,
Though purchased dear; tut, he will treble it
In some few terms, by his extorting wit.

When I, in simple meaning, went to sue
For tongue-tied Damus, that would needs go woo,
I prais'd him for his virtuous honest life.
"By God," cries Flora, "I'll not be his wife!
He'll ne'er come on." Now I swear solemnly,
When I go next I'll praise his villainy:
A better field to range in nowadays.
If vice be virtue, I can all men praise.

What, though pale Maurus paid huge simonies
For his half-dozen gelded vicaries,
Yet, with good honest cut-throat usury,
I fear he'll mount to reverent dignity.
"O sleight, all-canning sleight, all-damning sleight,
The only gally-ladder unto might."

Tuscus is trade-fall'n; yet great hope he'll rise,
For now he makes no count of perjuries;
Hath drawn false lights from pitch-black loveries,
Glazed his braided ware, cogs, swears, and lies;
Now since he hath the grace, thus graceless be,
His neighbours swear he'll swell with treasury.
Tut, who maintains such goods, ill-got, decay?

No, they'll stick by thy soul, they'll ne'er away.
Luscus, my lord's perfumer, had no sale
Until he made his wife a brothel-stale.
Absurd, the gods sell all for industry,
When what's not got by hell-bred villainy!

Codrus, my well-faced lady's tail-bearer
(He that sometimes play'th Flavia's usherer),
I heard one day complain to Lynceus
How vigilant, how right obsequious,
Modest in carriage, how true in trust,
And yet (alas!) ne'er guerdon'd with a crust.
But now I see he finds by his accounts
That sole Priapus, by plain-dealing, mounts.
How now? What, droops the new Pegasian inn?
I fear mine host is honest. Tut, begin
To set up whorehouse; ne'er too late to thrive;
By any means, at Porta Rich arrive;
Go use some sleight, or live poor Irus' life;
Straight prostitute thy daughter or thy wife,
And soon be wealthy; but be damn'd with it.
Hath not rich Milo then deep-reaching wit?
                                        Fair age!
When 'tis a high and hard thing t' have repute
Of a complete villain, perfect, absolute;
And roguing virtue brings a man defame,
A packstaff epithet, and scornèd name.

Fie, how my wit flags! How heavily
Methinks I vent dull sprightless poesy!
What cold black frost congeals my numbèd brain!
What envious power stops a satire's vein!
O now I know the juggling god of sleights,
With Caduceus nimble Hermes fights,
And mists my wit; offended that my rhymes
Display his odious world-abusing crimes.

O be propitious, powerful god of arts!
I sheathe my weapons, and do break my darts.
Be then appeased; I'll offer to thy shrine
An hecatomb of many spotted kine.
Myriads of beasts shall satisfy thy rage,
Which do profane thee in this apish age.
Infectious blood, ye gouty humours quake,
Whilst my sharp razor doth incision make.

Hem, nosti'n?

Curio, know'st me? Why, thou bottle-ale,
Thou barmy froth! O stay me, lest I rail
Beyond Nil ultra! to see this butterfly,
This windy bubble, task my balladry
With senseless censure. Curio, know'st my sprite?
Yet deem'st that in sad seriousness I write
Such nasty stuff as is Pygmalion?
Such maggot-tainted, lewd corruption!

Ha, how he glavers with his fawning snout,
And swears he thought I meant but faintly flout
My fine smug rhyme. O barbarous dropsy-noul!
Think'st thou that genius that attends my soul,
And guides my fist to scourge magnificos,
Will deign my mind be rank'd in Paphian shows?
Think'st thou that I, which was create to whip
Incarnate fiends, will once vouchsafe to trip
A pavin's traverse, or will lisp "Sweet love,"
Or pule "Aye me," some female soul to move?
Think'st thou that I in melting poesy
Will pamper itching sensuality
(That in the body's scum all fatally
Entombs the soul's most sacred faculty)?

Hence, thou misjudging censor: know I wrot
Those idle rhymes to note the odious spot
And blemish that deforms the lineaments
Of modern poesy's habiliments.
O that the beauties of invention,
For want of judgment's disposition,
Should all be spoil'd! O that such treasury,
Such strain of well-conceited poesy,
Should moulded be in such a shapeless form,
That want of art should make such wit a scorn!

Here's one must invocate some loose-legg'd dame,
Some brothel drab, to help him stanzas frame,
Or else (alas!) his wits can have no vent,
To broach conceit's industrious intent.
Another yet dares tremblingly come out;
But first he must invoke good Colin Clout.

Yon's one hath yean'd a fearful prodigy,
Some monstrous misshapen balladry;

His guts are in his brains, huge jobbernoul,
Right gurnet's-head; the rest without all soul.
Another walks, is lazy, lies him down,
Thinks, reads, at length some wonted sleep doth crown
His new-fall'n lids, dreams; straight, ten pound to one,
Out steps some fairy with quick motion,
And tells him wonders of some flow'ry vale;
Awakes, straight rubs his eyes, and prints his tale.

Yon's one whose strains have flown so high a pitch,
That straight he flags and tumbles in a ditch.
His sprightly hot high-soaring poesy
Is like that dreamèd of imagery,
Whose head was gold, breast silver, brassy thigh,
Lead legs, clay feet; O fair-framed poesy!

Here's one, to get an undeserved repute
Of deep deep learning, all in fustian suit
Of ill passed, far-fetch'd words attiereth
His period, that sense forsweareth.

Another makes old Homer Spenser cite,
Like my Pygmalion, where, with rare delight,
He cries, "O Ovid!" This caus'd my idle quill,
The world's dull ears with such lewd stuff to fill,
And gull with bumbast lines the witless sense
Of these odd nags, whose pates' circumference
Is fill'd with froth. O these same buzzing gnats
That sting my sleeping brows, these Nilus' rats,
Half dung, that have their life from putrid slime—
These that do praise my loose lascivious rhyme!
For these same shades, I seriously protest,
I slubbered up that chaos indigest,
To fish for fools that stalk in goodly shape;
"What, though in velvet cloak, yet still an ape."
Capro reads, swears, scrubs, and swears again,
"Now by my soul an admirable strain;"
Strokes up his hair, cries, "Passing passing good;"
O, there's a line incends his lustful blood!

Then Muto comes, with his new glass-set face,
And with his late-kiss'd hand my book doth grace,
Straight reads, then smiles, and lisps, "'Tis pretty good,"
And praiseth that he never understood.
But room for Flaccus, he'll my Satires read;
O how I trembled straight with inward dread!
But when I saw him read my fustian,
And heard him swear I was a Pythian,

Yet straight recall'd, and swears I did but quote
Out of Xylinum to that margent's note,
I could scarce hold and keep myself conceal'd,
But had well-nigh myself and all reveal'd.
Then straight comes Friscus, that neat gentleman,
That new-discarded academian,
Who, for he could cry Ergo in the school,
Straightway with his huge judgment dares control
Whatsoe'er he views: "That's pretty, pretty good;
That epithet hath not that sprightly blood
Which should enforce it speak; that's Persius' vein;
That's Juvenal's; here's Horace' crabbèd strain;"
Though he ne'er read one line in Juvenal,
Or, in his life, his lazy eye let fall
On dusky Persius. O, indignity
To my respectless free-bred poesy!

Hence, ye big-buzzing little-bodied gnats,
Ye tattling echoes, huge-tongued pigmy brats:
I mean to sleep: wake not my slumb'ring brain
With your malignant, weak, detracting vein.

What though the sacred issue of my soul
I here expose to idiots' control;
What though I bare to lewd opinion,
Lay ope to vulgar profanation,
My very genius,—yet know, my poesy
Doth scorn your utmost, rank'st indignity;

My pate was great with child, and here 'tis eased;
Vex all the world, so that thyself be pleased.

SATIRE VII

A Cynic Satire.

A man, a man, a kingdom for a man!
Why, how now, currish, mad Athenian?
Thou Cynic dog, see'st not the streets do swarm
With troops of men? No, no: for Circe's charm
Hath turn'd them all to swine. I never shall
Think those same Samian saws authentical:
But rather, I dare swear, the souls of swine
Do live in men. For that same radiant shine—
That lustre wherewith Nature's nature decked
Our intellectual part—that gloss is soiled

With staining spots of vile impiety,
And muddy dirt of sensuality.
These are no men, but apparitions,
Ignes fatui, glowworms, fictions,
Meteors, rats of Nilus, fantasies,
Colosses, pictures, shades, resemblances.
                                    Ho, Lynceus!
Seest thou yon gallant in the sumptuous clothes,
How brisk, how spruce, how gorgeously he shows?
Note his French herring-bones: but note no more,
Unless thou spy his fair appendant whore,
That lackies him. Mark nothing but his clothes,
His new-stamp'd compliment, his cannon oaths;
Mark those: for naught but such lewd viciousness
E'er gracèd him, save Sodom beastliness.
Is this a man? Nay, an incarnate devil,
That struts in vice and glorieth in evil.

A man, a man! Peace, Cynic, yon is one:
A complete soul of all perfection.
What, mean'st thou him that walks all open-breasted,
Drawn through the ear, with ribands, plumy-crested;
He that doth snort in fat-fed luxury,
And gapes for some grinding monopoly;
He that in effeminate invention,
In beastly source of all pollution,
In riot, lust, and fleshly seeming sweetness,
Sleeps sound, secure, under the shade of greatness?
Mean'st thou that senseless, sensual epicure—
That sink of filth, that guzzel most impure—
What, he? Lynceus, on my word thus presume,
He's nought but clothes, and scenting sweet perfume;
His very soul, assure thee, Lynceus,
Is not so big as is an atomus:
Nay, he is spriteless, sense or soul hath none,
Since last Medusa turn'd him to a stone.
A man, a man! Lo, yonder I espy
The shade of Nestor in sad gravity.
Since old Silenus brake his ass's back,
He now is forc'd his paunch and guts to pack
In a fair tumbrel. Why, sour satirist,
Canst thou unman him? Here I dare insist
And soothly say, he is a perfect soul,
Eats nectar, drinks ambrosia, sans control;
An inundation of felicity
Fats him with honour and huge treasury.
Canst thou not, Lynceus, cast thy searching eye,
And spy his imminent catastrophe?

He's but a sponge, and shortly needs must leese
His wrong-got juice, when greatness' fist shall squeeze
His liquor out. Would not some shallow head,
That is with seeming shadows only fed,
Swear yon same damask-coat, yon garded man,
Were some grave sober Cato Utican?
When, let him but in judgment's sight uncase,
He's naught but budge, old gards, brown fox-fur face;
He hath no soul the which the Stagyrite
Term'd rational: for beastly appetite,
Base dunghill thoughts, and sensual action,
Hath made him lose that fair creation.
And now no man, since Circe's magic charm
Hath turn'd him to a maggot that doth swarm
In tainted flesh, whose foul corruption
Is his fair food: whose generation
Another's ruin. O Canaan's dread curse,
To live in people's sins! Nay, far more worse,
To muck rank hate! But, sirra Lynceus,
Seest thou that troop that now effronteth us?
They are naught but eels, that never will appear
Till that tempestuous winds or thunder tear
Their slimy beds. But prithee stay a while;
Look, yon comes John-a-Noke and John-a-Stile;
They are nought but slow-paced, dilatory pleas,
Demure demurrers, still striving to appease
Hot zealous love. The language that they speak
Is the pure barbarous blacksaunt of the Gete;
Their only skill rests in collusions,
Abatements, stoppels, inhibitions.
Heavy-paced jades, dull-pated jobbernouls,
Quick in delays, checking with vain controls
Fair Justice' course; vile necessary evils,
Smooth-seeming saints, yet damn'd incarnate devils.

Far be it from my sharp satiric muse,
Those grave and reverent legists to abuse,
That aid Astræa, that do further right;
But these Megeras that inflame despite,
That broach deep rancour, that study still
To ruin right, that they their paunch may fill
With Irus' blood—these furies I do mean,
These hedgehogs, that disturb Astrea's scene.

A man, a man! Peace, Cynic, yon's a man;
Behold yon sprightly dread Mavortian;
With him I stop thy currish barking chops.—
What, mean'st thou him that in his swaggering slops

Wallows unbracèd, all along the street;
He that salutes each gallant he doth meet
With "Farewell, sweet captain, kind heart, adieu;"
He that last night, tumbling thou didst view
From out the great man's head, and thinking still
He had been sentinel of warlike Brill,
Cries out, "Que va la? zounds, que?" and out doth draw
His transform'd poniard, to a syringe straw,
And stabs the drawer? What, that ringo-root!
Mean'st thou that wasted leg, puff bumbast boot;
What, he that's drawn and quarterèd with lace;
That Wesphalian gammon clove-stuck face?
Why, he is nought but huge blaspheming oaths,
Swart snout, big looks, misshapen Switzers' clothes;
Weak meagre lust hath now consumèd quite,
And wasted clean away his martial sprite;
Enfeebling riot, all vices' confluence,
Hath eaten out that sacred influence
Which made him man.
That divine part is soak'd away in sin,
In sensual lust, and midnight bezelling,
Rank inundation of luxuriousness
Have tainted him with such gross beastliness,
That now the seat of that celestial essence
Is all possess'd with Naples' pestilence.
Fat peace, and dissolute impiety,
Have lullèd him in such security,
That now, let whirlwinds and confusion tear
The centre of our state; let giants' rear
Hill upon hill; let western termagant
Shake heaven's vault: he, with his occupant,
Are cling'd so close, like dew-worms in the morn,
That he'll not stir till out his guts are torn
With eating filth. Tubrio, snort on, snort on,
Till thou art waked with sad confusion.

Now rail no more at my sharp cynic sound,
Thou brutish world, that in all vileness drown'd
Hast lost thy soul: for nought but shades I see—
Resemblances of men inhabit thee.

Yon tissue slop, yon holy-crossèd pane,
Is but a water-spaniel that will fawn,
And kiss the water, whilst it pleasures him;
But being once arrivèd at the brim,
He shakes it off.
Yon in the cap'ring cloak, a mimic ape,
That only strives to seem another's shape.

Yon's Æsop's ass; yon sad civility
Is but an ox that with base drudgery
Ears up the land, whilst some gilt ass doth chaw
The golden wheat, he well apaid with straw.

Yon's but a muckhill overspread with snow,
Which with that veil doth even as fairly show
As the green meads, whose native outward fair
Breathes sweet perfumes into the neighbour air.

Yon effeminate sanguine Ganymede
Is but a beaver, hunted for the bed.

Peace, Cynic; see, what yonder doth approach;
A cart? a tumbrel? No, a badged coach.
What's in't? Some man. No, nor yet womankind,
But a celestial angel, fair, refined.
The devil as soon! Her mask so hinders me,
I cannot see her beauty's deity.
Now that is off, she is so vizarded,
So steep'd in lemon's juice, so surphulèd,
I cannot see her face. Under one hood
Two faces; but I never understood
Or saw one face under two hoods till now:
'Tis the right resemblance of old Janus' brow.
Her mask, her vizard, her loose-hanging gown
(For her loose-lying body), her bright-spangled crown,
Her long slit sleeve, stiff busk, puff verdingal,
Is all that makes her thus angelical.
Alas! her soul struts round about her neck;
Her seat of sense is her rebato set;
Her intellectual is a feignèd niceness,
Nothing but clothes and simpering preciseness.

Out on these puppets, painted images,
Haberdashers' shops, torchlight maskeries,
Perfuming-pans, Dutch ancients, glow-worms bright,
That soil our souls, and damp our reason's light!
Away, away, hence, coachman, go enshrine
Thy new-glazed puppet in port Esquiline!
Blush, Martia, fear not, or look pale, all's one;
Margara keeps thy set complexion.
Sure I ne'er think those axioms to be true,
That souls of men from that great soul ensue,
And of his essence do participate
As 'twere by pipes; when so degenerate,
So adverse is our nature's motion

To his immaculate condition,
That such foul filth from such fair purity,
Such sensual acts from such a Deity,
Can ne'er proceed. But if that dream were so,
Then sure the slime, that from our souls do flow,
Have stopp'd those pipes by which it was convey'd,
And now no human creatures, once disray'd
Of that fair gem.
Beasts' sense, plants' growth, like being as a stone;
But out, alas! our cognisance is gone.

PROEMIUM IN LIBRUM TERTIUM

In serious jest, and jesting seriousness,
I strive to scourge polluting beastliness;
I invocate no Delian deity,
No sacred offspring of Mnemosyne;
I pray in aid of no Castalian muse,
No nymph, no female angel, to infuse
A sprightly wit to raise my flagging wings,
And teach me tune these harsh discordant strings.
I crave no sirens of our halcyon times,
To grace the accents of my rough-hew'd rhymes;
But grim Reproof, stern hate of villainy,
Inspire and guide a Satire's poesy.
Fair Detestation of foul odious sin,
In which our swinish times lie wallowing,
Be thou my conduct and my genius,
My wits-inciting sweet-breath'd Zephyrus.
O that a Satire's hand had force to pluck
Some floodgate up, to purge the world from muck!
Would God I could turn Alpheus river in,
To purge this Augean oxstall from foul sin!
Well, I will try; awake, Impurity,
And view the veil drawn from thy villainy!

SATIRE VIII

Inamorato, Curio.

Curio, aye me! thy mistress' monkey's dead;
Alas, alas, her pleasure's burièd!
Go, woman's slave, perform his exequies,
Condole his death in mournful elegies.

Tut, rather pæans sing, hermaphrodite;
For that sad death gives life to thy delight.

Sweet-faced Corinna, deign the riband tie
Of thy cork-shoe, or else thy slave will die:
Some puling sonnet tolls his passing bell,
Some sighing elegy must ring his knell,
Unless bright sunshine of thy grace revive
His wambling stomach, certes he will dive
Into the whirlpool of devouring death,
And to some mermaid sacrifice his breath.
Then oh, oh then, to thy eternal shame,
And to the honour of sweet Curio's name,
This epitaph, upon the marble stone,
Must fair be graved of that true-loving one:

"Here lieth he, he lieth here,
That bounced and pity cried:
The door not oped, fell sick, alas,
Alas, fell sick and died!"

What Myrmidon, or hard Dolopian,
What savage-minded rude Cyclopian,
But such a sweet pathetic Paphian
Would force to laughter? Ho, Amphitrion,
Thou art no cuckold. What, though Jove dallièd,
During thy wars, in fair Alcmena's bed,
Yet Hercules, true born, that imbecility
Of corrupt nature, all apparently
Appears in him. O foul indignity!
I heard him vow himself a slave to Omphale,
Puling "Aye me!" O valour's obloquy!
He that the inmost nooks of hell did know,
Whose ne'er-crazed prowess all did overthrow,
Lies streaking brawny limbs in weak'ning bed;
Perfumed, smooth-kemb'd, new glazed, fair surphulèd.
O that the boundless power of the soul
Should be subjected to such base control!

Big-limb'd Alcides, doff thy honour's crown,
Go spin, huge slave, lest Omphale should frown.
By my best hopes, I blush with grief and shame
To broach the peasant baseness of our name.

O, now my ruder hand begins to quake,
To think what lofty cedars I must shake;
But if the canker fret, the barks of oaks,
Like humbler shrubs, shall equal bear the strokes

Of my respectless rude satiric hand.

Unless the Destin's adamantine band
Should tie my teeth, I cannot choose, but bite,
To view Mavortius metamorphos'd quite,
To puling sighs, and into "Aye me's" state,
With voice distinct, all fine articulate,
Lisping, "Fair saint, my woe compassionate;
By heaven! thine eye is my soul-guiding fate."

The god of wounds had wont on Cyprian couch
To streak himself, and with incensing touch
To faint his force, only when wrath had end;
But now, 'mong furious garboils, he doth spend
His feebled valour, in tilt and tourneying,
With wet turn'd kisses, melting dallying.
A pox upon't that Bacchis' name should be
The watchword given to the soldiery!
Go, troop to field, mount thy obscurèd fame,
Cry out St. George, invoke thy mistress' name;
Thy mistress and St. George, alarum cry!
Weak force, weak aid, that sprouts from luxury!

Thou tedious workmanship of lust-stung Jove,
Down from thy skies, enjoy our females' love:
Some fifty more Beotian girls will sue
To have thy love, so that thy back be true.

O, now me thinks I hear swart Martius cry,
Swooping along in wars' feign'd maskery;
By Lais' starry front he'll forthwith dye
In clutter'd blood, his mistress' livery;
Her fancy's colours waves upon his head.
O, well-fenced Albion, mainly manly sped,
When those that are soldadoes in thy state
Do bear the badge of base, effeminate,
Even on their plumy crests; brutes sensual,
Having no spark of intellectual!
Alack! what hope, when some rank nasty wench
Is subject of their vows and confidence?

Publius hates vainly to idolatrise
And laughs that Papists honour images;
And yet (O madness!) these mine eyes did see
Him melt in moving plaints, obsequiously
Imploring favour; twining his kind arms,
Using enchantments, exorcisms, charms;
The oil of sonnets, wanton blandishment,

The force of tears, and seeming languishment,
Unto the picture of a painted lass!
I saw him court his mistress' looking-glass,
Worship a busk-point, which, in secresy,
I fear was conscious of strange villainy;
I saw him crouch, devote his livelihood,
Swear, protest, vow peasant servitude
Unto a painted puppet; to her eyes
I heard him swear his sighs to sacrifice.
But if he get her itch-allaying pin,
O sacred relic! straight he must begin
To rave outright,—then thus: "Celestial bliss,
Can Heaven grant so rich a grace as this?
Touch it not (by the Lord! sir), 'tis divine!
It once beheld her radiant eye's bright shine!
Her hair embraced it. O thrice-happy prick,
That there was throned, and in her hair didst stick!"
Kiss, bless, adore it, Publius, never lin;
Some sacred virtue lurketh in the pin.

O frantic, fond, pathetic passion!
Is't possible such sensual action
Should clip the wings of contemplation?
O can it be the spirit's function,
The soul, not subject to dimension,
Should be made slave to reprehension
Of crafty nature's paint? Fie! can our soul
Be underling to such a vile control?

Saturio wish'd himself his mistress' busk,
That he might sweetly lie, and softly lusk
Between her paps; then must he have an eye
At either end, that freely might descry
Both hills and dales. But, out on Phrigio,
That wish'd he were his mistress' dog, to go
And lick her milk-white fist! O pretty grace!
That pretty Phrigio begs but Pretty's place.
Parthenophil, thy wish I will omit,
So beastly 'tis I may not utter it.
But Punicus, of all I'll bear with thee,
That fain wouldst be thy mistress' smug monkey.
Here's one would be a flea (jest comical!);
Another, his sweet lady's verdingal,
To clip her tender breech; another, he
Her silver-handled fan would gladly be;
Here's one would be his mistress' necklace, fain
To clip her fair, and kiss her azure vein.
Fond fools, well wish'd, and pity but 't should be;

For beastly shape to brutish souls agree.

If Laura's painted lip do deign a kiss
To her enamour'd slave, "O Heaven's bliss!"
(Straight he exclaims) "not to be match'd with this!"
Blaspheming dolt! go threescore sonnets write
Upon a picture's kiss, O raving sprite!

I am not sapless, old, or rheumatic,
No Hipponax, misshapen stigmatic,
That I should thus inveigh 'gainst amorous sprite
Of him whose soul doth turn hermaphrodite;
But I do sadly grieve, and inly vex,
To view the base dishonour of our sex.

Tush! guiltless doves, when gods, to force foul rapes,
Will turn themselves to any brutish shapes;
Base bastard powers, whom the world doth see
Transform'd to swine for sensual luxury!
The son of Saturn is become a bull,
To crop the beauties of some female trull.
Now, when he hath his first wife Metis sped,
And fairly choked, lest foul gods should be bred
Of that fond mule; Themis, his second wife,
Hath turn'd away, that his unbridled life
Might have more scope; yet, last, his sister's love
Must satiate the lustful thoughts of Jove.
Now doth the lecher in a cuckold's shape,
Commit a monstrous and incestuous rape.
Thrice sacred gods! and O thrice blessèd skies,
Whose orbs include such virtuous deities!

What should I say? Lust hath confounded all;
The bright gloss of our intellectual
Is foully soil'd. The wanton wallowing
In fond delights, and amorous dallying,
Hath dusk'd the fairest splendour of our soul;
Nothing now left but carcass, loathsome, foul;
For sure, if that some sprite remainèd still,
Could it be subject to lewd Lais' will?

Reason, by prudence in her function,
Had wont to tutor all our action,
Aiding, with precepts of philosophy,
Our feeblèd natures' imbecility;
But now affection, will, concupiscence,
Have got o'er reason chief pre-eminence.
'Tis so; else how should such vile baseness taint

As force it be made slave to nature's paint?
Methinks the spirit's Pegase, Fantasy,
Should hoise the soul from such base slavery;
But now I see, and can right plainly show
From whence such abject thoughts and actions grow.

Our adverse body, being earthly, cold,
Heavy, dull, mortal, would not long enfold
A stranger inmate, that was backward still
To all his dungy, brutish, sensual will:
Now hereupon our intellectual,
Compact of fire all celestial,
Invisible, immortal, and divine,
Grew straight to scorn his landlord's muddy slime;
And therefore now is closely slunk away
(Leaving his smoky house of mortal clay),
Adorn'd with all his beauty's lineaments
And brightest gems of shining ornaments,
His parts divine, sacred, spiritual,
Attending on him; leaving the sensual
Base hangers-on lusking at home in slime,
Such as wont to stop port Esquiline.
Now doth the body, led with senseless will
(The which, in reason's absence, ruleth still),
Rave, talk idly, as 'twere some deity,
Adoring female painted puppetry;
Playing at put-pin, doting on some glass
(Which, breath'd but on, his falsèd gloss doth pass);
Toying with babies, and with fond pastime,
Some children's sport, deflow'ring of chaste time;
Employing all his wits in vain expense,
Abusing all his organons of sense.

Return, return, sacred Synderesis!
Inspire our trunks! Let not such mud as this
Pollute us still. Awake our lethargy,
Raise us from out our brain-sick foolery!

SATIRE IX

Here's a Toy to mock an Ape indeed.

Grim-faced Reproof, sparkle with threatening eye!
Bend thy sour brows in my tart poesy!
Avaunt! ye curs, howl in some cloudy mist,
Quake to behold a sharp-fang'd satirist!

O how on tip-toes proudly mounts my muse!
Stalking a loftier gait than satires use.
Methinks some sacred rage warms all my veins,
Making my sprite mount up to higher strains
Than well beseems a rough-tongu'd satire's part;
But Art curbs Nature, Nature guideth Art.

Come down, ye apes, or I will strip you quite,
Baring your bald tails to the people's sight!
Ye mimic slaves, what, are you perch'd so high?
Down, Jackanapes, from thy feign'd royalty!
What! furr'd with beard—cast in a satin suit,
Judicial Jack? How hast thou got repute
Of a sound censure? O idiot times,
When gaudy monkeys mow o'er spritely rhymes!
O world of fools! when all men's judgment's set,
And rests upon some mumping marmoset!
Yon Athens' ape (that can but simp'ringly
Yaul "Auditores humanissimi!"
Bound to some servile imitation,
Can, with much sweat, patch an oration)
Now up he comes, and with his crookèd eye
Presumes to squint on some fair poesy;
And all as thankless as ungrateful Thames,
He slinks away, leaving but reeking steams
Of dungy slime behind. All as ingrate
He useth it as when I satiate
My spaniel's paunch, who straight perfumes the room
With his tail's filth: so this uncivil groom,
Ill-tutor'd pedant, Mortimer's numbers
With muck-pit Esculine filth bescumbers.
Now the ape chatters, and is as malcontent
As a bill-patch'd door, whose entrails out have sent
And spewed their tenant.

My soul adores judicial scholarship;
But when to servile imitatorship
Some spruce Athenian pen is prenticèd,
'Tis worse than apish. Fie! be not flatterèd
With seeming worth! Fond affectation
Befits an ape, and mumping babion.
O what a tricksy, learnèd, nicking strain
Is this applauded, senseless, modern vein!
When late I heard it from sage Mutius' lips,
How ill, methought, such wanton jigging skips
Beseem'd his graver speech. "Far fly thy fame,
Most, most of me beloved! whose silent name
One letter bounds. Thy true judicial style

I ever honour; and, if my love beguile
Not much my hopes, then thy unvalued worth
Shall mount fair place, when apes are turnèd forth."

I am too mild. Reach me my scourge again;
O yon's a pen speaks in a learned vein,
Deep, past all sense. Lanthorn and candle-light!
Here's all invisible—all mental sprite!
What hotch-potch gibberidge doth the poet bring?
How strangely speaks, yet sweetly doth he sing?
I once did know a tinkling pewterer,
That was the vilest stumbling stutterer
That ever hack'd and hew'd our native tongue,
Yet to the lute if you had heard him sung,
Jesu! how sweet he breath'd! You can apply.
O senseless prose, judicial poesy,
How ill you're link'd! This affectation,
To speak beyond men's apprehension,
How apish 'tis, when all in fustian suit
Is cloth'd a huge nothing, all for repute
Of profound knowledge, when profoundness knows
There's naught contain'd but only seeming shows!

Old Jack of Paris-garden, canst thou get
A fair rich suit, though foully run in debt?
Look smug, smell sweet, take up commodities,
Keep whores, fee bawds, belch impious blasphemies,
Wallow along in swaggering disguise,
Snuff up smoke-whiffs, and each morn, 'fore she rise,
Visit thy drab? Canst use a false-cut die
With a clean grace and glib facility?
Canst thunder cannon-oaths, like th' rattling
Of a huge, double, full-charg'd culvering?
Then Jack, troop 'mong our gallants, kiss thy fist,
And call them brothers; say a satirist
Swears they are thine in near affinity,
All cousin-germans, save in villainy;
For (sadly, truth to say) what are they else
But imitators of lewd beastliness?
Far worse than apes; for mow or scratch your pate,
It may be some odd ape will imitate;
But let a youth that hath abused his time
In wrongèd travel, in that hotter clime,
Swoop by old Jack, in clothes Italianate,
And I'll be hang'd if he will imitate
His strange fantastic suit-shapes:
Or let him bring o'er beastly luxuries,
Some hell-devisèd lustful villanies,

Even apes and beasts would blush with native shame,
And think it foul dishonour to their name,
Their beastly name, to imitate such sin
As our lewd youths do boast and glory in.

Fie! whither do these monkeys carry me?
Their very names do soil my poesy.
Thou world of marmosets and mumping apes,
Unmask, put off thy feignèd, borrowed shapes!
Why looks neat Curus all so simp'ringly?
Why babblest thou of deep divinity,
And of that sacred testimonial,
Living voluptuous like a bacchanal?
Good hath thy tongue; but thou, rank Puritan,
I'll make an ape as good a Christian;
I'll force him chatter, turning up his eye,
Look sad, go grave; demure civility
Shall seem to say, "Good brother, sister dear!"
As for the rest, to snort in belly-cheer,
To bite, to gnaw, and boldly intermel
With sacred things, in which thou dost excel,
Unforced he'll do. O take compassion
Even on your souls! Make not Religion
A bawd to lewdness. Civil Socrates,
Clip not the youth of Alcibiades
With unchaste arms. Disguisèd Messaline,
I'll tear thy mask, and bare thee to the eyn
Of hissing boys, if to the theatres
I find thee once more come for lecherers,
To satiate (nay, to tire) thee with the use
Of weak'ning lust. Ye feigners, leave t' abuse
Our better thoughts with your hypocrisy;
Or, by the ever-living verity!
I'll strip you nak'd, and whip you with my rhymes,
Causing your shame to live to after-times.

SATIRE X

Satira Nova.

Stultorum plena sunt omnia.

TO HIS VERY FRIEND, MASTER E. G.

From out the sadness of my discontent,
Hating my wonted jocund merriment

(Only to give dull time a swifter wing),
Thus scorning scorn, of idiot fools I sing.
I dread no bending of an angry brow,
Or rage of fools that I shall purchase now;
Who'll scorn to sit in rank of foolery,
When I'll be master of the company?
For prithee, Ned, I prithee, gentle lad,
Is not he frantic, foolish, bedlam mad,
That wastes his sprite, that melts his very brain
In deep designs, in wit's dark gloomy strain?
That scourgeth great slaves with a dreadless fist,
Playing the rough part of a satirist,
To be perused by all the dung-scum rabble
Of thin-brain'd idiots, dull, incapable,
For mimic apish scholars, pedants, gulls,
Perfumed inamoratos, brothel-trulls?
Whilst I (poor soul) abuse chaste virgin time,
Deflow'ring her with unconceived rhyme.
"Tut, tut; a toy of an idle empty brain,
Some scurril jests, light gewgaws, fruitless, vain,"
Cries beard-grave Dromus; when, alas! God knows
His toothless gums ne'er chaw but outward shows.
Poor budge-face, bowcase sleeve: but let him pass;
"Once fur and beard shall privilege an ass."

And tell me, Ned, what might that gallant be,
Who, to obtain intemperate luxury,
Cuckolds his elder brother, gets an heir,
By which his hope is turnèd to despair?
In faith (good Ned), he damn'd himself with cost;
For well thou know'st full goodly land was lost.

I am too private. Yet methinks an ass
Rhymes well with viderit utilitas;
Even full as well, I boldly dare aver,
As any of that stinking scavenger
Which from his dunghill be dedaubèd on
The latter page of old Pygmalion.
O that this brother of hypocrisy
(Applauded by his pure fraternity)
Should thus be puffèd, and so proud insist
As play on me the epigrammatist!
"Opinion mounts this froth unto the skies,
Whom judgment's reason justly vilifies."
For (shame to the poet) read, Ned, behold
How wittily a master's hood can scold!

An Epigram which the Author Vergidemiarum caused to be pasted to the latter page of every Pygmalion that came to the Stationers of Cambridge.

I ask'd Physicians what their counsel was
For a mad dog, or for a mankind ass?
They told me, though there were confections' store
Of poppy-seed and sovereign hellebore,
The dog was best cured by cutting and kinsing,
The ass must be kindly whipped for winsing.
Now then, S. K., I little pass.
Whether thou be a mad dog or a mankind ass.

Smart jerk of wit! Did ever such a strain
Rise from an apish schoolboy's childish brain?
Dost thou not blush, good Ned, that such a scent
Should rise from thence, where thou hadst nutriment?
"Shame to Opinion, that perfumes his dung,
And streweth flowers rotten bones among!
Juggling Opinion, thou enchanting witch!
Paint not a rotten post with colours rich."
But now this juggler, with the world's consent,
Hath half his soul; the other, compliment;
Mad world the whilst. But I forget me, I,
I am seducèd with this poesy,
And, madder than a bedlam, spend sweet time
In bitter numbers, in this idle rhyme.
Out on this humour! From a sickly bed,
And from a moody mind distemperèd,
I vomit forth my love, now turn'd to hate,
Scorning the honour of a poet's state.
Nor shall the kennel rout of muddy brains
Ravish my muse's heir, or hear my strains,
Once more. No nitty pedant shall correct
Enigmas to his shallow intellect
Enchantment, Ned, have ravishèd my sense
In a poetic vain circumference.
Yet thus I hope (God shield I now should lie),
Many more fools, and most more wise than I.

Humours.

Sleep, grim Reproof; my jocund muse doth sing
In other keys, to nimbler fingering.
Dull-sprighted Melancholy, leave my brain—

To hell, Cimmerian night! in lively vein
I strive to paint, then hence all dark intent
And sullen frowns! Come, sporting Merriment,
Cheek-dimpling Laughter, crown my very soul
With jouisance, whilst mirthful jests control
The gouty humours of these pride-swoll'n days,
Which I do long until my pen displays.
O, I am great with Mirth! some midwif'ry,
Or I shall break my sides at vanity.
Room for a capering mouth, whose lips ne'er stir
But in discoursing of the graceful slur.
Who ever heard spruce skipping Curio
E'er prate of ought but of the whirl on toe,
The turn-above-ground, Robrus' sprawling kicks,
Fabius' caper, Harry's tossing tricks?
Did ever any ear e'er hear him speak
Unless his tongue of cross-points did entreat?
His teeth do caper whilst he eats his meat,
His heels do caper whilst he takes his seat;
His very soul, his intellectual
Is nothing but a mincing capreal.
He dreams of toe-turns; each gallant he doth meet
He fronts him with a traverse in the street.
Praise but Orchestra, and the skipping art,
You shall command him, faith you have his heart
Even cap'ring in your fist. A hall, a hall!
Room for the spheres, the orbs celestial
Will dance Kempe's jig: they'll revel with neat jumps;
A worthy poet hath put on their pumps.
O wit's quick traverse, but sance ceo's slow;
Good faith 'tis hard for nimble Curio.
"Ye gracious orbs, keep the old measuring;
All's spoil'd if once ye fall to capering."

Luscus, what's play'd to-day? Faith now I know
I set thy lips abroach, from whence doth flow
Naught but pure Juliet and Romeo.
Say who acts best? Drusus or Roscio?
Now I have him, that ne'er of ought did speak
But when of plays or players he did treat—
Hath made a common-place book out of plays,
And speaks in print: at least what e'er he says
Is warranted by Curtain plaudities.
If e'er you heard him courting Lesbia's eyes,
Say (courteous sir), speaks he not movingly,
From out some new pathetic tragedy?
He writes, he rails, he jests, he courts (what not?),
And all from out his huge long-scraped stock

Of well-penn'd plays.

Oh come not within distance! Martius speaks,
Who ne'er discourseth but of fencing feats,
Of counter times, finctures, sly passatas,
Stramazones, resolute stoccatas,
Of the quick change with wiping mandritta,
The carricada, with the embrocata.

"Oh, by Jesu, sir!" methinks I hear him cry,
"The honourable fencing mystery
Who doth not honour?" Then falls he in again,
Jading our ears, and somewhat must be sain
Of blades and rapier-hilts, of surest guard,
Of Vincentio, and the Burgonian's ward.

This bombast foil-button I once did see,
By chance, in Livia's modest company;
When, after the god-saving ceremony,
For want of talk-stuff, falls to foinery;
Out goes his rapier, and to Livia
He shows the ward by puncta reversa,
The incarnata. Nay, by the blessed light!
Before he goes, he'll teach her how to fight
And hold her weapon. Oh I laugh amain,
To see the madness of this Martius' vein!

But room for Tuscus, that jest-mounging youth
Who ne'er did ope his apish gerning mouth
But to retail and broke another's wit
Discourse of what you will, he straight can fit
Your present talk, with "Sir, I'll tell a jest"
(Of some sweet lady, or grand lord at least).
Then on he goes, and ne'er his tongue shall lie
Till his engrossèd jests are all drawn dry;
But then as dumb as Maurus, when at play
Hath lost his crowns, and pawn'd his trim array.
He doth nought but retail jests: break but one,
Out flies his table-book; let him alone,
He'll have it i'faith. Lad, hast an epigram,
Wilt have it put into the chaps of fame?
Give Tuscus copies; sooth, as his own wit
(His proper issue) he will father it.
O that this echo, that doth seek, spet, write
Nought but the excrements of others sprite,
This ill-stuff'd trunk of jests (whose very soul
Is but a heap of gibes) should once enroll
His name 'mong creatures termed rational!

Whose chief repute, whose sense, whose soul and all
Are fed with offal scraps, that sometimes fall
From liberal wits in their large festival.

Come aloft, Jack! room for a vaulting skip,
Room for Torquatus, that ne'er oped his lip
But in prate of pommado reversa,
Of the nimble, tumbling Angelica.
Now, on my soul, his very intellect
Is nought but a curvetting sommerset.

"Hush, hush," cries honest Philo, "peace, desist!
Dost thou not tremble, sour satirist,
Now that judicial Musus readeth thee?
He'll whip each line, he'll scourge thy balladry,
Good faith he will." Philo, I prithee stay
Whilst I the humour of this dog display.
He's nought but censure; wilt thou credit me,
He never writ one line in poesy,
But once at Athens in a theme did frame
A paradox in praise of virtue's name;
Which still he hugs and lulls as tenderly
As cuckold Tisus his wife's bastardy?
Well, here's a challenge: I flatly say he lies
That heard him ought but censure poesies;
'Tis his discourse, first having knit the brow,
Stroke up his fore-top, champèd every row,
Belcheth his slavering censure on each book
That dare presume even on Medusa look.

I have no artist's skill in symphonies,
Yet when some pleasing diapason flies
From out the belly of a sweet-touch'd lute,
My ears dare say 'tis good: or when they suit
Some harsher sevens for variety,
My native skill discerns it presently.
What then? Will any sottish dolt repute,
Or ever think me Orpheus absolute?
Shall all the world of fidlers follow me,
Relying on my voice in musickry?

Musus, here's Rhodes; let's see thy boasted leap,
Or else avaunt, lewd cur, presume not speak,
Or with thy venom-sputtering chaps to bark
Gainst well-penn'd poems, in the tongue-tied dark.

O for a humour, look, who yon doth go,
The meagre lecher, lewd Luxurio!

'Tis he that hath the sole monopoly,
By patent, of the suburb lechery;
No new edition of drabs comes out,
But seen and allow'd by Luxurio's snout.
Did ever any man e'er hear him talk,
But of Pick-hatch, or of some Shoreditch balk,
Aretine's filth, or of his wand'ring whore;
Of some Cinædian, or of Tacedore;
Of Ruscus' nasty, loathsome brothel rhyme,
That stinks like A-jax froth, or muck-pit slime?
The news he tells you is of some new flesh,
Lately broke up, span new, hot piping fresh.
The courtesy he shows you is some morn
To give you Venus 'fore her smock be on.
His eyes, his tongue, his soul, his all, is lust,
Which vengeance and confusion follow must.
Out on this salt humour, letcher's dropsy,
Fie! it doth soil my chaster poesy!

O spruce! How now, Piso, Aurelius' ape,
What strange disguise, what new deformèd shape,
Doth hold thy thoughts in contemplation?
Faith say, what fashion art thou thinking on?
A stitch'd taffeta cloak, a pair of slops
Of Spanish leather? O, who heard his chops
E'er chew of ought but of some strange disguise?
This fashion-monger, each morn 'fore he rise,
Contemplates suit-shapes, and once from out his bed,
He hath them straight full lively portrayèd.
And then he chucks, and is as proud of this
As Taphus when he got his neighbour's bliss.
All fashions, since the first year of this queen,
May in his study fairly drawn be seen;
And all that shall be to his day of doom;
You may peruse within that little room;
For not a fashion once dare show his face,
But from neat Piso first must take his grace:
The long fool's coat, the huge slop, the lugg'd boot,
From mimic Piso all do claim their root.
O that the boundless power of the soul
Should be coop'd up in fashioning some roll!

But O, Suffenus! (that doth hug, embrace
His proper self, admires his own sweet face;
Praiseth his own fair limbs' proportion,
Kisseth his shade, recounteth all alone
His own good parts) who envies him? Not I,
For well he may, without all rivalry.

Fie! whither's fled my sprite's alacrity?
How dull I vent this humorous poesy!
In faith I am sad, I am possess'd with ruth,
To see the vainness of fair Albion's youth;
To see their richest time even wholly spent
In that which is but gentry's ornament;
Which, being meanly done, becomes them well;
But when with dear time's loss they do excell,
How ill they do things well! To dance and sing,
To vault, to fence, and fairly trot a ring
With good grace, meanly done, O what repute
They do beget! But being absolute,
It argues too much time, too much regard
Employ'd in that which might be better spar'd
Than substance should be lost. If one should sue
For Lesbia's love, having two days to woo,
And not one more, and should employ those twain
The favour of her waiting-wench to gain,
Were he not mad? Your apprehension,
Your wits are quick in application.
Gallants,
Methinks your souls should grudge and inly scorn
To be made slaves to humours that are born
In slime of filthy sensuality.
That part not subject to mortality
(Boundless, discursive apprehension
Giving it wings to act his function),
Methinks should murmur when you stop his course,
And soil his beauties in some beastly source
Of brutish pleasures; but it is so poor,
So weak, so hunger-bitten, evermore
Kept from his food, meagre for want of meat,
Scorn'd and rejected, thrust from out his seat,
Upbraid by capons' grease, consumèd quite
By eating stews, that waste the better sprite,
Snibb'd by his baser parts, that now poor soul
(Thus peasanted to each lewd thought's control)
Hath lost all heart, bearing all injuries,
The utmost spite and rank'st indignities,
With forcèd willingness; taking great joy,
If you will deign his faculties employ
But in the mean'st ingenious quality.
(How proud he'll be of any dignity!)
Put it to music, dancing, fencing-school,
Lord, how I laugh to hear the pretty fool,
How it will prate! His tongue shall never lie,
But still discourse of his spruce quality,

Egging his master to proceed from this,
And get the substance of celestial bliss.
His lord straight calls his parliament of sense;
But still the sensual have pre-eminence.
The poor soul's better part so feeble is,
So cold and dead is his Synderesis,
"That shadows, by odd chance, sometimes are got;
But O the substance is respected not!"
Here ends my rage. Though angry brow was bent,
Yet I have sung in sporting merriment.

TO EVERLASTING OBLIVION

Thou mighty gulf, insatiate cormorant!
Deride me not, though I seem petulant
        To fall into thy chops. Let others pray
        For ever their fair poems flourish may;
But as for me, hungry Oblivion,
Devour me quick, accept my orison,
        My earnest prayers, which do importune thee,
        With gloomy shade of thy still empery,
        To veil both me and my rude poesy.
Far worthier lines, in silence of thy state,
Do sleep securely, free from love or hate;
From which this living ne'er can be exempt,
But whilst it breathes will hate and fury tempt:
Then close his eyes with thy all-dimming hand,
Which not right glorious actions can withstand.
Peace, hateful tongues, I now in silence pace,
Unless some hound do wake me from my place,
        I with this sharp, yet well-meant poesy,
        Will sleep secure, right free from injury
        Of canker'd hate, or rankest villainy.

TO HIM THAT HATH PERUSED ME

Gentle or ungentle hand that holdest me, let not thine eye be cast upon privateness, for I protest I glance not on it. If thou hast perused me, what lesser favour canst thou grant than not to abuse me with unjust application? Yet, I fear me, I shall be much, much injuried by two sorts of readers: the one being ignorant, not knowing the nature of a satire (which is, under feigned private names to note general vices), will needs wrest each feigned name to a private unfeigned person: the other, too subtile, bearing a private malice to some greater personage than he dare, in his own person, seem to malign, will strive, by a forced application of my general reproofs, to broach his private hatred,—than the which I know not a greater injury can be offered to a satirist. I durst presume, knew they how guiltless and how free I

were from prying into privateness, they would blush to think how much they wrong themselves in seeking to injure me. Let this protestation satisfy our curious searchers; so may I obtain my best hopes, as I am free from endeavouring to blast any private man's good name. If any one (forced with his own guilt) will turn it home and say, "'Tis I," I cannot hinder him; neither do I injure him. For other faults of poesy, I crave no pardon, in that I scorn all penance the bitterest censurer can impose upon me. Thus (wishing each man to leave inquiring whom I am, and learn to know himself) I take a solemn congee of this fusty world.
THERIOMASTIX.

ENTERTAINMENT OF ALICE, DOWAGER-COUNTESS OF DERBY

The noble Lorde & Lady of Huntingdons Entertainement of theire right Noble Mother Alice: Countesse Dowager of Darby the first night of her honors arrivall att the house of Ashby.

TO THE RIGHT NOBLE LADY ALICE, COUNTESS-DOWAGER OF DERBY

Madam,
If my slight Muse may suit your noble merit,
My hopes are crown'd, and I shall cheer my spirit;
But if my weak quill droops or seems unfit,
'Tis not your want of worth, but mine of wit.
The servant of your honour'd virtues,

John Marston.

When her Ladyship approached the Park corner, a full noise of cornets winded; and when she entered into the Park, treble cornets reported one to another, as giving warning of her Honour's nearer approach; when presently her eye was saluted with an antique gate, which suddenly was erected in this form. Upon the gate did hang many silver scrolls with this word in them, Tantum uni. Upon the battlements over the gate three gilt shields in diamond-figure, impaled on the top with three coronets purfled with gold, and severally inscribed with silver words; in the first shield, Venisti tandem; in the second, Nostra sera; in the third, Et sola voluptas. Over these, upon a half sphere, stood embossed an antique figure gilt; the slight towers to this gate, which were only raised for show, were set out with battlements, shields, and coronets suitable to the rest. When the Countess came near the gate an old enchantress in crimson velvet, with pale face, black hair, and disliking countenance, affronted her Ladyship, and thus rudely saluted her:—

Woman, Lady, Princess, Nymph, or Goddess,
For more you are not, and you seem no less;
Stay, and attempt not passage through this port,
Here the pale Lord of Sadness keeps his court,
Rough-visag'd Saturn, on whose bloodless cheeks,
Dull Melancholy sits, who straightly seeks

To seize on all that enter through this gate.
Grant gracious listening, and I shall relate
The means, the manner, and of all the sense,
Whilst your fair eye enforceth eloquence.
There was a time (and since that time the sun
Hath not yet through nine signs of heaven run)
When the high Sylvan, that commands these woods,
And his bright Nymph, fairer than Queen of Floods,
With most impatient longings hoped to view
Her face to whom their hearts' dear'st zeal was due.
Youth's joys to love, sweet light unto the blind,
Beauty to virgins, or what wit can find
Most dearly wished, was not so much desired
As she to them; O my dull soul is fired
To tell their longings, but it is a piece
That would o'erload the famous tongues of Greece.
Yet long they hop'd, till Rumour struck Hope dead,
And showed their wishes were but flatterèd;
For scarce her chariot cut the easy earth,
And journeyed on, when Winter with cold breath
Crosseth her way, her borrowed hair doth shine
With glittering icicles all crystalline;
Her brows were periwigg'd with softer snow,
Her russet mantle, fringed with ice below,
Sat stiffly on her back; she thus came forth,
Ushered with tempest of the frosty North;
And seeing her, she thought she sure had seen
The sweet-breath'd Flora, the bright Summer's Queen.
So full of cheerful grace she did appear,
That Winter feared her face recalled the year,
And forced untimely springs to seize her right,
Whereat with anger and malicious spite
She vows revenge; straight with tempestuous wings,
From Taurus, Alps, and Scythian rocks she flings
Their covering off, and here their thick fur spread,
That patient earth was almost smotherèd.
Up Boreas mounts, and doth so strongly blow
Athwart her way huge drifts of blinding snow,
That mountain-like, at length heaps rose so high,
Man's sight might doubt whether Heaven or Earth were sky.
Hereat she turnèd back, and left her way
(Necessity all mortals must obey);
Which was no sooner voiced and hither flown,
It sads me but to think what grief was shown;
Which to augment (mishap ne'er single falls),
The God of Sadness and of Funerals,
Of heavy pensiveness and discontent,
Cold and dull Saturn hither straight was sent.

Myself, Merimna, who still wait upon
Pale Melancholy and Desolation,
Usher'd him in, when straight we strongly seize
All this sad house, and vowed no means should ease
These heavy bands which pensive Saturn tied,
Till with wish'd grace this house was beautified.
Pace then no further, for vouchsafe to know,
Till her approach here can no comfort grow;
'Tis only one can their sad bondage break,
Whose worth I may admire, not dare to speak.
She's so complete, that her much honoured state
Gives Fortune Virtue, makes Virtue fortunate;
As one in whom three rare mix'd virtues sit
Seen seldom joinèd, Fortune, Beauty, Wit;
To this choice Lady and to her dear state
All hearts do open, as alone this gate;
She only drives away dull Saturn hence,
She whom to praise I need her eloquence!

This speech thus ended, presently Saturn issued from forth the port, and curiously beholding the Countess, spake thus:—

Peace! stay, it is, it is, it is even she!
Hail happy honours of Nobility!
Did never Saturn see, or ne'er see such?
What should I style you? what choice phrase may touch,
Or hopes in words such wondrous grace to suit,
Whose worth doth want an equal attribute.
Let never mortal wondering silence break,
Since to express you Gods themselves must speak.
Sweet glories of your sex, know that your eyes
Makes mild the roughest planet of the skies.
Even we, the Lord that sits on ebon thrones,
Circled with sighs and discontented groans,
Are forced at your fair presence to relent,
At your approach all Saturn's force is spent.
Now breaks my bands, now sadness leaves their towers,
Now all are turn'd to Flora's smiling bowers;
Then now give way, now is my bondage due
Only to those who safely envy you.
Hence, solitary Beldam, sink to-night,
I give up all to joy, and to delight.
And now pass on, all-happy-making dame!
O could you but imagine what a flame
Of many joys now in their bosoms shine
Who count it their dear'st honour to be thine,
You would aver, to number them who seeks
Must sure invent some new arithmetics,

For who to cast their reckoning takes in hand
Had need for counters take the ocean-sand.
Their service is your right, your love their due
Who only love themselves for loving you.
Their palace waits you with so hearty gate
Men cannot utter nor Gods scarce relate.

Then passed the whole troop to the house, until the Countess had mounted the stairs to the great chamber; on the top of which, Merimna, having changed her habit all to white, met her, and, whilst a consort softly played, spake thus:—

Madam,
See what a change the spirit of your eyes
Hath wrought in us. Hence dull Saturn flies,
And we that were the ghost of woe and earth
Are all transform'd unto the soul of mirth.
O we are full of joy, no breast more light
But those who owe you theirs by nature's right;
From whom vouchsafe this present,—'tis a work
Wherein strange miracles and wonders lurk.

For, know, that Lady whose ambition towers
Only to this, to be term'd worthy yours;
Whose forehead I could crown with clearest rays,
But that her praise is she abhors much praise;
Not long since thought she saw in slumb'ring trances
The Queen of Fairies and of moonlight dances
Come tripping in; and with a fairy kiss
She chastely touch'd her and straight gave her this
With this strange charge:—"This piece alone was made
For her in whom no graces e'er shall fade;
For her whose worth is such I dare aver
It fears not satire nor the flatterer;
For her who gave you first most gracing name,
Who loveth goodness for itself, not fame;
For her whom modest virtue doth enfold so
That she had rather be much graced than told so;
For her for whom, had you the whole world's breast
And of it all gave her sole interest,
You'd judge it slight." This said, hence straight she flew,
And left it her who only vows it you.
Then whilst our breast with secret welcomes ring,
Vouchsafe acceptance of this offering.

Thus with a song Merimna presented her honour with a very curious and rich waistcoat; which done, the Countess passed on to her chamber.

The Masque presented by four knights and four gentlemen at the right noble Earl of Huntingdon's house of Ashby in honour of his Lady's most worthy mother's arrival, Alice Countess Dowager of Derby. The form was thus:—

At the approach of the countesses into the great chamber the hoboys played until the room was marshalled; which once ordered, a traverse slided away; presently a cloud was seen move up and down almost to the top of the great chamber, upon which Cynthia was discovered riding; her habit was blue satin, fairly embroidered with stars and clouds: who looking down and earnestly surveying the ladies, spake thus:—

CYNTHIA
Are not we Cynthia? and shall earth display
Brighter than us and force untimely day?
What daring flames beam such illustrious light,
Enforcing darkness from the claim of night?
Up, Ariadne, thy clear beauty rouse,
Thou Northern Crown to lusty Bacchus' spouse,
Let's mix our glories to outblaze your flame;
To be outshone is Heaven's and great hearts' shame.
Look down; know'st them? See how their fronts rebate
Splendour like Jove and beauty worth our state!
Hath our bright brother, the fair Lord of days,
Into their eyes shed his us-dark'ning rays?
Or hath some daring spirit forgot Jove's ire
And to grace them stol'n his celestial fire?
We are not Phœbe, this is not Heaven's story;
Place gives not worth, but worth gives place his glory.

In the midst of this speech Ariadne rose from the bottom of the room, mounted upon a cloud which waved up until it came near Cynthia, where resting Ariadne spake thus:—

ARIADNE
Can our chaste queen, searching Apollo's sister,
Not know those stars that in yon valley glister?
Is virtue strange to heaven? Can Cynthia
Not know the goodly-form'd Pasithea?
She who loves greatness to be greatly good,
Knowing fair'st worth from virtue springs, not blood;
Whose graceful just proportion is held such
That what may be judged beauty must have touch
And proof from hers: yet this her least of grace
(Which is the most in most)—her beauty's but the case
Of fairest mind: when Fortune gave her eyes,
Her worth made Fortune judge she once had eyes.
But see a piece that would strike envy blind,
Whose face would Furies tame, make monsters kind.
He gave her mighty praise and yet no other
But that in mind and form she's like her mother:

Up, raisèd passion, and with pæans follow
Grace of the Muses, daughter of Apollo!
O precious selahs' praise thy worth is under;
He that would limn thy grace must only wonder.

Then views not Cynthia sweet Sophrosyne,
Long honour of most rare virginity,
But now much happy in her noble choice?
In well-link'd nuptials all the gods rejoice.

Next learn'd Eulogia, bright in gracious rays,
Whose merit faster springeth than my praise;
For whoso strives to give her worth fair due,
Shall find his praise straight old, her merit new.

CYNTHIA
But, look, whose eyes are those that shine more clear
Than lightning thrown from shield of Jupiter?
See, see, how quick fire leaps from forth her eyes
Which burn all hearts and warm the very skies.
Is't not bright Euthera?

ARIADNE
The very same,
But her mind's splendour hath a nobler flame.
But let the gods Eurythia behold,
And let them envy her, face nobly bold,
Proportion all proportion, with a mind
But like itself, no epithet can find.

CYNTHIA
Let's visit them and slide from our abode:
Who loves not virtue leaves to be a god.
Sound, spheres, spread your harmonious breath,
When mortals shine in worth gods grace the earth.

The clouds descend: while soft music soundeth, **CYNTHIA** and **ARIADNE** dismount from their clouds,
and, pacing up to the ladies, **CYNTHIA**, perceiving **ARIADNE** wanting her crown of stars, speaks thus:—

CYNTHIA
But where is Ariadne's wreath of stars,
Her eight pure fires that stud with golden bars
Her shining brows? hath sweet-tongued Mercury
Advanced his sons to station of the sky
And throned them in thy wreath? or dost thou leave
Thy splendour off and trust of gods deceive?

ARIADNE

Queen of chaste dew, they will not be confined
Or fix themselves where Mercury assign'd,
But every night upon a forest-side,
On which an eagle percheth, they abide,
And honour her with their most raisèd light,
Chaste sports, just praises, and all soft delight,
Vowing their beams to make her presence heaven:
Thus is the glory of my front bereaven.

CYNTHIA
Tell them they err, and say that we, the Queen
Of night's pale lamps, have now the substance seen
Whose shadow they adore. Go, bring those eight
At mighty Cynthia's summons hither straight.
Let us behold, that mount whilst we salute,
Their faces, 'fore whom no dullness can be mute.

Presently **ARIADNE** sings this short call:—

Music and gentle night,
Beauty, youth's chief delight,
Pleasures all full invite
Your due attendance to this glorious room;
Then, if you have or wit or virtue, come,
Oh, come! oh, come!

Suddenly, upon this song, the cornets were winded, and the traverse that was drawn before the masquers sank down. The whole show presently appeareth, which presented itself in this figure: the whole body of it seemed to be the side of a steeply ascending wood, on the top of which, in a fair oak, sat a golden eagle, under whose wings sat, in eight several thrones, the **EIGHT MASQUERS**, with visards like stars, their helms like Mercury's, with the addition of fair plumes of carnation and white, their antique doublets and other furniture suitable to those colours, the place full of shields, lights, and **PAGES** all in blue satin robes, embroidered with stars. The **MASQUERS**, thus discovered, sat still until **ARIADNE** pronounced this invocation, at which they descended:—

ARIADNE
Mercurian issue, sons of son of Jove,
By the Cyllenian rod, and by the love
Devotely chaste you vow Pasithea,
Descend: first thou more bright of these
That givest my crown her name, clear Dolopes,
Whose brave descent lets not thy fair heart fall
As born of parents most heroical,
Who vows himself, his life, his sword and fortune
To her whose constant goodness doth importune
More than he is: descend! Next him, Auctolius,
Of nimble spirit slide to honour us;
Faithfull'st Evander; clear-soul'd Erythus;

The hopeful Prilis and sweet Polybus;
And thou, true son of quick-brain'd Mercury,
Dear-loved Myrtillus, with that bright soul mix'd,
Experienced Lares, that at last is fix'd
After much danger in securer sphere.
Here all with wishèd easiness appear,
And O, if ever you were worth the grace
Of viewing majesty in mortal's face,
If e'er to perfect worth you vow'd heart's duty,
Show spirit worth your virtues and their beauty.

The violins upon this played a new measure, to which the masquers danced; and ceasing, **CYNTHIA**
spake:—

Stay a little, and now breathe ye,
Whilst these ladies grace bequeath ye;
Then mix fair hands, and gently ease ye,
Cynthia charms hence what may displease ye.
From ladies that are rudely coy,
Barring their loves from modest joy,
From ignorant silence, and proud looks,
From those that answer out of books,
From those that hate our chaste delight,
I bless the fortune of each starry Knight.
From gallants who still court with oaths,
From those whose only grace is clothes,
From bumbast stockings, vile leg-makers,
From beards and great tobacco-takers,
I bless the fortune of each starry dame.
Sing, that my charm may be more strong;
The gods are bound by verse and song.

The Song

Audacious night makes bold the lip,
Now all court chaster pleasure,
Whilst to Apollo's harp you trip,
And tread the gracing measure.
CYNTHIA
Now meet, now break, then feign a warlike sally

So Cynthia sports, and so the gods may dally.
Lascivious youth not dare to speak
The language of loose city;
He that Diana's bonds doth break
Is held most rudely witty.
CYNTHIA
Now meet, now break, then feign a warlike sally
So Cynthia sports, and so the gods may dally.

Judicious wit, now raise thy brain,
Now heat thy nimbler spirit,
Show what delicious faces strain;
Much passion shows much merit.
CYNTHIA
Now meet, now break, then feign a warlike sally;

So Cynthia sports, and so the gods may dally.
Disgracious dullness yet much mars
The shape of courtly talking;
He that can silent touch such stars
His soul lies in his walking.
CYNTHIA
Now meet, now break, then feign a warlike sally;
So Cynthia sports, and so the gods may dally.

During this song, the **MASQUERS** presented their shields, and took forth their **LADIES** to dance. After they had danced many measures, galliards, corantos, and levaltos, the night being much spent, whilst the masquers prepared themselves for their departing measure, **CYNTHIA** spake thus:—

CYNTHIA
Now pleasing rest; for, see the night
(Wherein pale Cynthia claims her right)
Is almost spent; the morning grows,
The rose and violet she strows
Upon the high celestial floor,
'Gainst Phœbus rise from paramour.
The Fairies, that my shades pursue,
And bathe their feet in my cold dew,
Now leave their ringlets and be quiet,
Lest my brother's eye should spy it.
Then now let every gracious star
Avoid at sound of Phœbus' car;
Into your proper place retire,
With bosoms full of beauty's fire;
Hence must slide the Queen of Floods,
For day begins to gild the woods.
Then whilst we sing, though you depart,
I'll swear that here you leave your heart.

The eclogue which a despairing **SHEPHERD** spake to a **NYMPH** at my Lady's departure:—

Stay, fair Beliza, and, whilst Heaven throws
On the crack'd earth
His burning breath,
O hear thy Dorus' woes,
Whose cause and cure only Beliza knows.

See now the god of flames in full pomp rides,
And now each lass
On flowery grass
By the cool fountain sides
With quiet bosom and soft ease abides.

Do you so too, for see this bounteous spring:
Pray thee sit down,
Then shall I crown
Thy brows with flowery ring,
Whilst thus with shepherd's homely voice I sing.

He sang a passionate ditty; which done, he spake thus:—

SHEPHERD

Now, fairest, deign once to impart,
Did ever live so coy a lass
Who unto love was never moved?

NYMPH
Yes, shepherd, she that hath the heart
And is resolved her life to pass
Neither to love or be beloved.

SHEPHERD
She senseless lives without affection.

NYMPH
Yet happy lives without subjection.

SHEPHERD
To be pluck'd are roses blown,
To be mow'd are meadows grown sown,
Gems are made but to be shown,
And woman's best—

NYMPH
To keep her own.

SHEPHERD
Well, shepherdess, still hate to love me;
No scorn from my fix'd vow shall move me.
When sheep to finest grass have loathing,
When courtiers shall disdain rich clothing,
When shepherds shun their mayday's sports,
Green sickness when 'tis rife in courts,—
O then, and not till then, I'll hate
Beliza, my sole love and fate.

NYMPH
When love in daughters shall ascend
For simple Piety's sole end,
When any child her mother graces
With all she can, yet all defaces
In her fair thought the faith she oweth
(Though what she can she freely showeth);
Then, shepherd, mayst thou hope attend,
For then my hate shall have an end.

SHEPHERD
Thou'rt mine, Beliza; for behold
    All the hopes thy wishes crave,
    All the best the world can have,

Here these happy characters unfold;
Which who dares but once deny,
    In the most just and fair defence
    Of her love's highest excellence,
I of thousands am the weak'st will die:
From which, O deign to give this touch,
Who gives what he can get, gives much.

[The **SHEPHERD** presented a scarf.

Farewell, farewell!
Joy, Love, Peace, Health in you long dwell,
With our farewell, farewell!

So the **COUNTESS** passed on until she came through the little park, where **NIOBE** presented her with a cabinet and so departed.

John Marston – A Short Biography

John Marston was born to John and Maria Marston née Guarsi, and baptised on October 7th, 1576 at Wardington, Oxfordshire. His father was an eminent lawyer of the Middle Temple who first practiced in London and then became the counsel to Coventry and later its steward.

Marston entered Brasenose College, Oxford in 1592 and earned his BA in 1594. By 1595, he was in London, living in the Middle Temple. His interests were in poetry and play writing, although his father's will of 1599 hopes that he would not further pursue such vanities.

His brief career in literature began with a foray into the then fashionable genres of erotic epyllion and satire; erotic plays for boy actors to be performed before educated young men and members of the inns of court.

In 1598, he published 'The Metamorphosis of Pigmalion's Image and Certaine Satyres', a book of poetry in imitation of, on the one hand, Ovid, and, on the other, the Satires of Juvenal. He also published 'The Scourge of Villanie', in 1598. (these were issued under the pseudonym "W. Kinsayder.") The satire in these books is even more savage and misanthropic than the prevailing norm for other satirists of the era. Marston's style sometimes bends to the point of unintelligibility: he believed that satire should be rough and obscure. Marston seems to have been enraged by Joseph Hall's claim to be the first satirist in English; Hall comes in for some indirect retribution later in one or more of his satires. Some see William Shakespeare's Thersites and Iago, as well as the mad speeches of King Lear as influenced by 'The Scourge of Villanie'.

Marston had, however, arrived on the literary scene as the fad for verse satire was coming under pressure from the authority's censors. Both the Archbishop of Canterbury and the Bishop of London banned 'The Scourge of Villanie' had it publicly burned, along with copies of works by other satirists, on 4th June 1599.

In September 1599, John Marston began to work for the famed Philip Henslowe as a playwright. Marston proved a good match for the private stage where boy players performed racy dramas for an audience of city gallants and young members of the Inns of Court.

'Histriomastix' has been regarded as his first play; performed by either the Children of Paul's or the students of the Middle Temple in around 1599. Its performance kicked off an episode in literary history commonly known as the 'War of the Theatres'; the literary feud between Marston, Jonson and Dekker that took place between 1599 and 1602.

Around 1600, Marston wrote 'Jack Drum's Entertainment' and 'Antonio and Mellida', and in 1601 he wrote 'Antonio's Revenge', a sequel to the latter play; all three were performed by the company at Paul's. In 1601, he contributed poems to Robert Chester's 'Love's Martyr'. For Henslowe, he may have also collaborated with Dekker, Day, and Haughton on 'Lust's Dominion'.

By 1601, he was well known in London literary circles, particularly in his role as enemy to the equally brilliant and difficult Ben Jonson. Jonson, who reported that Marston had accused him of sexual profligacy, satirized Marston as Clove in 'Every Man Out of His Humour', as Crispinus in 'Poetaster', and as Hedon in 'Cynthia's Revels'. Jonson thought Marston a false poet, a vain, careless writer who plagiarised the works of others and whose works were marked by bizarre diction and ugly neologisms. For his part, Marston used Jonson as the complacent, arrogant critic Brabant Senior in 'Jack Drum's Entertainment' and as the envious, misanthropic playwright and satirist Lampatho Doria in 'What You Will'.

'The Return from Parnassus (II)', an anonymous and satirical play performed at St. John's College, Cambridge in 1601 and 1602, characterised Marston as a poet whose writings see him 'pissing against the world'.

Jonson states that at one point their 'War' boiled over into the physical when he had beaten Marston and taken his pistol. However, the two playwrights were reconciled; Marston wrote a prefatory poem for Jonson's 'Sejanus' in 1605 and dedicated 'The Malcontent' to him.

Beyond this episode Marston's career continued to gather both strength, assets and followers. In 1603, he became a shareholder in the Children of Blackfriars company, at that time known for steadily pushing the boundaries of personal satire, violence, and lewdness on stage. He wrote and produced two plays with the company. The first was 'The Malcontent' in 1603, his most famous play. This work was originally written for the children at Blackfriars and was later taken over by the Kings' Men at the Globe, with additions by John Webster. His second play for the Blackfriars children was 'The Dutch Courtesan', a satire on lust and hypocrisy, in 1604-5.

In 1605, he worked with George Chapman and Ben Jonson on 'Eastward Ho', a satire of popular taste and the vain imaginings of wealth to be found in the colony of Virginia. Chapman and Jonson were arrested for, according to Jonson, a few clauses that offended the Scots, but Marston escaped any imprisonment. Their detainment was brief, and the charges were dropped.

He married Mary Wilkes in 1605, the daughter of the Reverend William Wilkes, one of the chaplains to King James.

In 1606, Marston seems to have had mixed fortunes with the king. At times offending and at others pleasing. In 'Parasitaster, or, The Fawn', he satirized the king specifically. However, in the summer of that year, he put on a production of 'The Dutch Courtesan' for the King of Denmark's visit, with a Latin verse on King James that was presented by hand to the king. Finally, in 1607, he wrote 'The Entertainment at Ashby', a masque for the Earl of Huntingdon.

Marston took the theatre world by surprise when he gave up writing plays in 1609 at the age of thirty-three. He sold his shares in the company of Blackfriars. His departure from the literary scene may have been because of further offence he gave to the king. The king suspended performances at Blackfriars and had Marston imprisoned.

After release he moved into his father-in-law's house to study philosophy. In 1609, he became a reader at the Bodleian library at Oxford. On 24th September he was made a deacon and then a priest on 24th December 1609. In October 1616, Marston was assigned the living of Christchurch, Hampshire.

He died (accounts vary) on either the 24th or 25th June 1634 in London and was buried in the Middle Temple Church.

Tombs at that time were often inscribed with 'Memoriae Sacrum' ('Sacred to the memory') and then the occupants name and a brief account of their achievements. According to Anthony à Wood Marston's tomb stone read 'Oblivioni Sacrum' ('Sacred to Oblivion'), which was probably composed by Marston, and both self-abasing and witty in upturning the tradition.

Marston's reputation through the centuries has varied widely, like that of most of the minor Renaissance dramatists. Both 'The Malcontent' and 'The Dutch Courtesan' remained on stage in altered forms throughout the Restoration.

After the Restoration, Marston's works were largely reduced to literary history. The general resemblance of 'The Malcontent' to 'Hamlet' and Marston's role in the 'War of the Theatres' ensured that his plays would receive some scholarly attention, but they were not performed, nor widely read.

The Romantic movement in English literature unevenly resuscitated Marston's reputation. In his lectures, William Hazlitt praised Marston's genius for satire; however, if the romantic critics were willing to grant Marston's best work a place among the great accomplishments of the age, they remained aware of his inconsistency, what Swinburne would later call his 'uneven and irregular demesne'.

In the twentieth century, however, a few critics were willing to consider Marston as a writer who was very much in control of the world he created. T. S. Eliot saw that this 'irregular demesne' was a part of Marston's world and that "It is ... by giving us the sense of something behind, more real than any of the personages and their action, that Marston establishes himself among the writers of genius".

John Marston – A Concise Bibliography

Plays and production dates

Histriomastix (play), 1599

Antonio and Mellida, London, Paul's theater, 1599–1600.
Jack Drum's Entertainment, London, Paul's theater, 1599/1600.
Antonio's Revenge, London, Paul's theater, 1600.
What You Will, London, Paul's theater, 1601.
The Malcontent, London, Blackfriars Theatre, 1603–1604; Globe Theatre, 1604.
Parasitaster, or The Fawn, London, Blackfriars theater, 1604.
Eastward Ho, by Marston, George Chapman, and Ben Jonson, London, Blackfriars theater, 1604–1605.
The Dutch Courtesan, London, Blackfriars theater, 1605.
The Wonder of Women, or The Tragedy of Sophonisba, London, Blackfriars theater, 1606.
The Spectacle Presented to the Sacred Majesties of Great Britain, and Denmark as They Passed through London, London, 31 July 1606.
The Entertainment of the Dowager-Countess of Darby, Ashby-de-la-Zouch in Leicestershire, 1607.
The Insatiate Countess, by Marston and William Barksted, London, Whitefriars Theatre, c 1608.

Books

The Metamorphosis of Pigmalions Image. And Certaine Satyres.
The Scourge of Villanie. Three Bookes of Satyres (1598; revised and enlarged edition, 1599)
Jacke Drums Entertainment: Or, The Comedie of Pasquill and Katherine (1601)
Loves Martyr: or, Rosalins Complaint, by Marston, Ben Jonson, William Shakespeare, and George Chapman (1601)
The History of Antonio and Mellida (1602)
Antonios Revenge (1602)
The Malcontent (1604)
Eastward Hoe, by Marston, Chapman, and Jonson (1605)
The Dutch Courtezan (1605)
Parasitaster, or The Fawne (1606)
The Wonder of Women, or The Tragedie of Sophonisba (1606)
What You Will (1607)
Histrio-mastix: Or, The Player Whipt (1610)
The Insatiate Countesse, by Marston and William Barksted (1613)
The Workes of Mr. J. Marston (1633); republished as Tragedies and Comedies (1633)
Comedies, Tragi-comedies; & Tragedies, Nonce Collection (1652)
Lust's Dominion, or The Lascivious Queen (probably the same play as The Spanish Moor's Tragedy), by Marston, Thomas Dekker, John Day, and William Haughton (1657)